MERSEYSIDE MEANDERS

Country Walks & Town Trails around Wirral, Liverpool and Southport

Michael Smout

Published by Sigma Leisure – an imprint of
Sigma Press, 1 South Oak Lane, Wilmslow, Cheshire SK9 6AR, England.

British Library Cataloguing in Publication Data
A CIP record for this book is available from the British Library.

ISBN: 1-85058-780-9

Photographs: Micael Smout, except where stated

Cover photographs: main picture, Liverpool Waterfront
(by courtesy of the Liverpool Daily Post and Echo);
smaller pictures, from top: the Chinatown area of Liverpool;
The church of St Nicholas, Whiston; Hadlow Road Station,
Willaston *(all by Michael Smout)*

Maps: Jeremy Semmens

Typesetting and Design by: Sigma Press, Wilmslow, Cheshire.

Cover Design: Sigma Press, Wilmslow and Design House, Marple Bridge

Printed by: MFP Design & Print

Preface

Preparing a book of walks can be a lonely task. It entails pouring over Ordnance Survey maps, plodding along previously unknown paths, retracing steps after getting lost, remembering to take photographs, getting the material onto the word processor before it is forgotten, drawing the walk maps, revising the material and checking the proofs. It is something of a miracle and relief to see the book appear at the end of this long process.

Every encouragement along the way is welcome. So my thanks are due to a number of such encouragers. To the members of the West Lancashire Ramblers Association who have always been ready to share their knowledge and expertise. To the congregation of St Michael's Church, Aughton who annually appear at the Ormskirk Bookshop on book-signing day to ensure that I am not too embarrassed by lack of custom. To Graham Beech and the staff at Sigma Press who have been brave enough to publish five of my books and still remain solvent. Finally to my wife Val for making sure that I do not go hungry on long expeditions.

Michael Smout

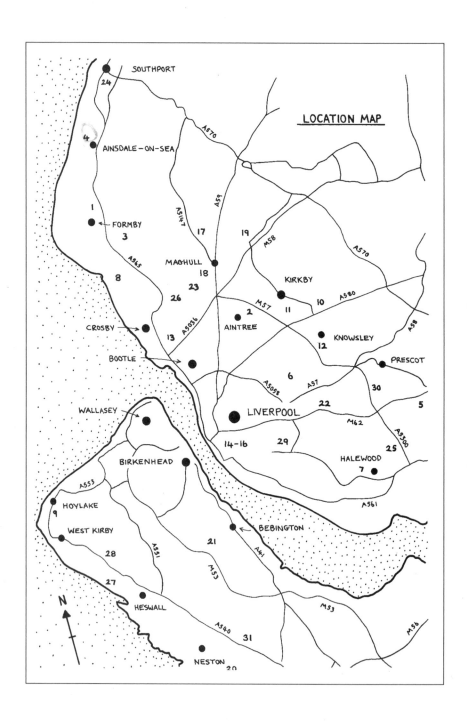

Contents

Introduction

Snide remarks about the area are stock-in-trade for many people who have never set foot on Merseyside. The impression that many outsiders seem to have is of a district of urban dereliction and despair. This is not the place to go into the successful regeneration story, only to note that some would think it impossible to produce a book of Merseyside walks. I hope that I can prove that the proposition is entirely untrue. The walks are mainly within the confines of the Wirral, Liverpool and Southport districts. A few are city walks, but most cross open land and fields. This means that a large population has a range of walks almost on the doorstep. Liverpool had one of the earliest walking groups in the country, long before the Ramblers Association was formed. So, the area has a history of walking.

Doctors tell us that taking regular exercise is vital to our health, and I hope this book will help to encourage Merseysiders to discover the benefits of walking. Merseyside has no mountains or high hills, though I hesitate to say that all the walks are flat – because all ground undulates. But all the walks come within the classification of 'Easy' – so there's no excuse for not getting out and enjoying the fresh air, countryside and many surprises that await you.

As in my previous books, I have put in as much directional information as possible for, in the course of time, changes do take place. The Merseyside local authorities and Merseyrail have all made efforts to encourage walking and have produced leaflets of walks. They are available from information offices and most libraries. The only pity is that one authority does not stock the others' leaflets.

If you find that you get through all the walks in the book and have not been posted missing, then there are other walks in the Merseyside area to be found in my other books: *West Lancashire Walks* includes walks in Crosby, Formby and Ince Blundell. In my *East Lancashire Walks*, there is an expedition to Hale and an additional walk in Cronton. It is also includes a walk in Halewood, which has been extended for inclusion in this book.

The appropriate Ordnance Survey Explorer map number is included in the text for each walk. It is suggested that an A-Z map might be helpful for town walks.

1. Ainsdale

Ainsdale's hills and sand dunes feature on this walk. On some stretches the path is pure sand, where it can be a bit harder going.

Route: Fisherman's Path – Ainsdale Hills – Ainsdale Sand Dunes – Fisherman's Path.

Starting Point: Freshfield Merseyrail Station. Grid reference: 292 083.

Distance: 5 miles.

Duration: 3 hours.

Map: Explorer 285.

By Train: Freshfield Station is on the Merseyrail Liverpool – Southport Northern Line.

By Car: Freshfield Station is in Victoria Road. There is usually room to park a car in the first part of Montagu Road next to the station car park.

Refreshments: Available at the shop by the station.

---

1. From Freshfield station, walk along Montagu Road, at the side of the car park. The road goes straight, on parallel to the railway. Then the bridleway runs between the road and the rails. As the bridleway comes back onto the road, pass the footpath sign pointing to Fisherman's Path. The fisherman theme is continued with Fisherman's Close on the right. After another bridleway sign, at the end of the tarmac road, continue straight on at the Freshfield Dune Heath sign, going along the stone track edged with short wooden posts. Do not follow the bridleway sign to the right.

At the 'Beach 1 mile' sign, turn left across the railway. Take great care because there have been accidents at this point in the past. The 'Samaritans' sign gives indication that some incidents here have not been accidental. Having watched for passing trains, the next things to watch for are flying golf balls. Keep an eye open as the path crosses Formby Golf Course.

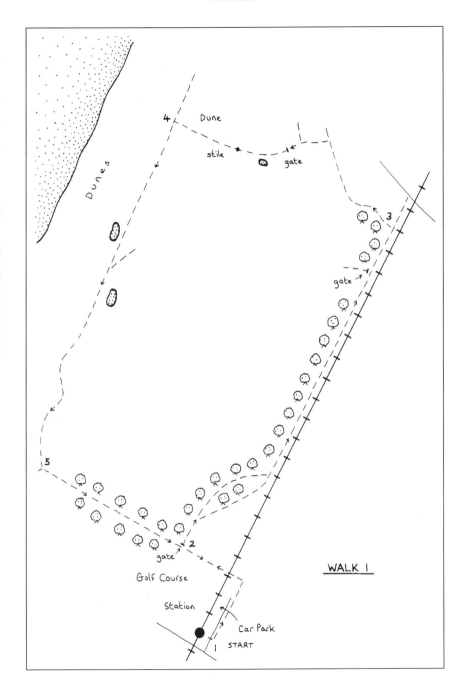

2. On reaching a gate and information point, turn right. You will see the first of a series of white-topped marker posts. These posts are placed along most of our route, being closer together on the dune section. Various unused buildings are passed, before going through a section of fir trees, passing a path that goes to the left. All the fir trees *en route* have had their lower branches lopped to enable vegetation to flourish on the ground below. The track bends left and uphill by the 'Formby Golf Club Keep Out' notice. The paths divide to meet again at a later point. We take the one to the left, which is the more interesting of the two and not open to bicycles. The sandy path soon turns sharp right. Ignore the cross path to go up on firmer ground through the fir trees. Follow round to the right at the white marker and downhill again, where there is a break in the trees on the right. Through more fir trees, the track bends sharply left at a point where there is a closed path opposite. It is not long before arriving at the junction with the other main path.

Turn left along the wide stone track. Across the grassed area to the right is the railway. Beyond that is Woodvale airfield. Stay on this track, avoiding all paths back into the woodland. After trees have closed in on the right as well as the left, go through a gate. You are now on a tarmac road. The sign to the left states 'Private. To Warden's Office and West End Lodge'. Walk straight ahead. Over to the right can be seen the road bridge over the railway. Look for a turning left onto a dirt track into the woods.

3. A wooden fence and white marker post are on the corner. The path goes up and down through the firs, then becoming entirely of sand. It passes by some silver birch trees, before a very short steep uphill section. From now on, follow the white markers. The path goes on through open ground to bend right through a sandy defile. After this, resist the temptation to follow a path up a sand dune. If you stay on the lower level, you will soon see another marker. This leads you on to the 'Ainsdale Sandhills' sign. Go through the gap in the wire fence adjacent to the sign. After a few metres of gorse, turn left off the main track along a narrower grass track, which brings you back along side the perimeter fence. As soon as this becomes a sand track again, turn left by the gate with a notice about keeping dogs on a lead. On this section of the route, there are no marker posts.

The narrow grass track stays on the right of the fence, only moving away from it to go round a small pond. Go through a kissing gate to continue on the path by the fence. This brings you up to a small tump of a sand dune. Take the short, steepish path to the top, (not the one that goes to the left of it) where you will find a white marker post. From here, you can see the beach and sea beyond the dunes. Down the other side of the dune, come into the small valley to reach a T-junction. A sign to the right tells you that this is the Dune Path. Shore Road 1 kilometres to the right.

The beach at Ainsdale

4. Turn left in the 2km direction. Another sign on the right informs that this is a breeding ground for the rare Natterjack toad.

From this point, follow the white markers again, as the path runs mainly through narrow sand valleys. A wire fence is passed on the left and next a fenced pond with a 'Keep Out' sign. With another wire fence to the left, the track splits for a few metres. It does not matter which one you follow. Now bear right towards another white marker, then on through the next narrow grassed valley. A 'Dune Repair Work' notice, followed by another referring to the toads are passed. Ignore a path coming in from the left as you continue along the valley. Then going higher, passing a few metres above a pond in the valley to the right, the surrounds become more grassy.

At the point where a path comes in from the left and another from the right, go straight on. On reaching the English Nature Reserve information notice, keep on the grass track on the right of the fence. This passes a pond, a stock grazing notice, then one explaining the reason for the clearance of pine trees. This latter action by English Nature received much opposition from local naturalists. When the fence ends, the path becomes sandy again. Away to the left, the ground has trees and shrubs, with woodland in the distance. The path passes through coarse grass, then along the edge of a sand dune. By the white marker, drop downhill toward another marker, which can sometimes be a little obscured by grass. Follow right towards the next way mark. Continue ahead up a sudden incline. The next marker cannot be seen until going over the brow, so do not walk round to the right before the incline. At the top, looking back, the beach can be seen not too far away. Go ahead to the English Nature sign. Turn left along the path.

5. At the T-junction, turn left again. Follow the broad track, which gradually makes its way uphill through woodland, until reaching the gate. From here, return on the outward route across the golf course and railway to turn right back to the station.

2. Aintree

The famous racecourse is part of the route, which also includes one or two of the older houses of Aintree Village. Please note that the path around the racecourse is closed during Grand National period plus other infrequent race meetings. For information ring Aintree Racecourse on 0151 523 2600.

Route: Handcock's Bridge – Aintree Racecourse – Bull Bridge – Leeds – Liverpool Canal – Handcock's Bridge.

Starting Point: The car park by Handcock's Canal Bridge on Wango Lane. Grid reference: 388 982.

Distance: 3 miles.

Duration: 1 hour or so.

Map: Explorer 275.

By Train: Old Roan station is on the Northern Merseyrail Liverpool to Ormskirk line. Cross the A59 dual carriage way. Bear right along Aintree Lane. The walk can be picked up at point 3 by the Anchor canal bridge.

By Car: From Old Roan station on the A59 Liverpool- Ormskirk Road, turn left at the traffic lights into Aintree Lane leading into School Lane. Wango Lane is first right after the Blue Anchor.

Refreshments: Blue Anchor, School Lane.

1. From the car park at Handcock's Bridge, go out through the car entrance. The bridge derives its name from a Mr Handcock, who lived in a nearby cottage. Lord Sefton gave him the job of opening and closing the bridge when necessary. Cross the road and go through the wooden chicane. Follow the track, with the old railway embankment on the left. Soon you are by the canal. Carry on towards the gates in front of you. As the canal swings to the right, take the narrow footpath to the left of the gates. On the right is the perimeter mesh fence of the racecourse. To left are the remains of the wooden railway fence. The small stream going across the course over to the right is Becher's Brook.

Captain Becher, formerly of the Buckinghamshire Yeomanry, became a professional jockey. In the first Grand National of 1839, he fell at the brook now named after him.

Passing the remains of an old station platform, stay by the perimeter fence. Stay by the fence, with open parkland to the left. If time allows, it is well worth while exploring the tracks of this newly designed area.

2. Faced by houses, turn right through the tall iron gateway. You are now on Aintree racecourse.

It was in 1827 that a flat racecourse was opened by William Lynn, the landlord of the Waterloo Hotel in Liverpool. In 1836, Lynn held a Grand Liverpool Steeplechase at Maghull. The winner was The Duke, whose rider was Captain Becher. After two more years at Maghull, the first Grand National was held at Aintree on 26 February 1839, although the actual name was not coined until eight years later. The course, as well as most of the rest of Aintree, was owned by Lord Sefton. In 1843, he leased the course to Edward Topham, a breeder of horses. It eventually passed to his grandson Arthur. Although he was not interested in racing, his wife Mirabel, an actress, was. In 1938, she became chairman of Topham Ltd. One of the great Liverpool characters, the grande dame was famous for her array of eye-catching headgear. Lord Sefton sold the course to Mrs Topham in 1949. Not for nothing was she known as the Queen of Aintree. By 1964, Topham Ltd. was in financial trouble. This was not surprising for a race course that was only used for three or four days a years. In 1974, she sold out to Bill Davies of the Walton Group. The race itself was organised by Ladbrokes, the bookmakers. The future of the course was secured for posterity, when it was bought by Racecourse Holdings on behalf of the Jockey Club.

3. Through the gate in the fence, you are faced by wooden palings. Turn right to follow the path between fences. You are walking parallel to the path on which you have just been. The path joins a wide track. Continue along it, until reaching a gate. From the gate, stay on

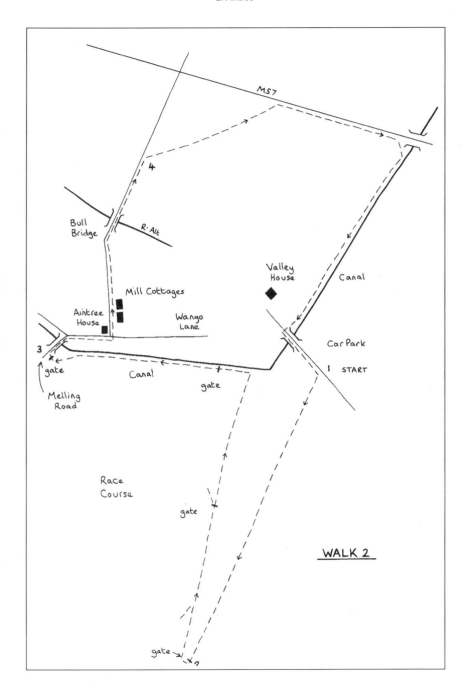

the right-hand side of the fence. On reaching the canal, turn left. The path now stays by the canal fence. It descends to reach a gate. Through the gate, carry on. Then ascend the wooden steps to pass a seat. After going down some more steps, you quickly go up some more. Pass another seat and down the final steps to level ground. The path starts to move away from the canal to arrive, through a gate, at Melling Road.

Turn right over Anchor Bridge, then right again along School Lane. On the right, pass the Blue Anchor pub, built on the site of an earlier one destroyed by fire in 1900. Opposite the Wango Lane corner is the 17th-century Aintree House.

This is a house with a history. At least two people of note were associated with it. In the middle of the 18th century, the printer John Sadler lived here. In 1757, he first printed the *Liverpool Chronicle*. After selling it, he next received a contract from Wedgwood to print on one of its new line in crockery. One of Sadler's workers was Richard Abbey, who founded the Herculaneum pottery company. He lived at Abbey Farm in Aintree Lane. Opposite to Aintree House are Kennel House and Cottage. At the end of the 19th century, the hunt had their kennels here. School Lane now becomes Bull Bridge Lane. Just before reaching Greenside Avenue on the left, look across to the right. Here is Mill Square, so unknown that it is not even mentioned on the Liverpool A-Z map. At the bottom of the entry are Mill Cottages. From the middle of the 18th century, these were farm cottages, which were built by Lord Sefton for the use of his farm workers. Carry on down the road. In the distance, high on its mound, can be seen the church of St Thomas and the Holy Rood, Melling. The last house on the right is an old village cottage. Bull Bridge, which was renovated in 1931, crosses the River Alt. Walk towards the motorway bridge.

4. Just before the sign that states that Melling welcomes careful drivers, turn right along the track, past the gate deterring motor cars. With the deeply sided stream to the right, the track heads towards the motorway. On reaching the Melling Water Treatment plant, go onto the grass track between the plant and the motorway. Fortunately, at this point the motorway is high up, heard but unseen. The path climbs through scrub land, veering away from the motorway.

Valley House

On nearing the canal, go left towards the motorway bridge onto the towpath. Turn right, continuing back towards Handcock's Bridge. Just before the bridge, Valley House can be seen across the field, partly hidden behind trees. Built in the mid-17th century with mullioned windows, it was originally a farm house. On reaching the bridge, turn left across the canal, back to the car park.

For more information see 'Aintree Past and Present' by Joan Harkins.

3. Altcar

Just outside the Merseyside boundary, the vast vistas of the land round Altcar village give a feeling of remoteness and mystery.

Route: St Michael's Church – Engine Lane – Altcar Moss – St Michael's Church.

Starting Point: St Michael's Church, Great Altcar. Grid reference 320 067.

Map: Explorer 285.

Distance: 4 miles.

Duration: 2 hours.

By Car: From the A565 Liverpool – Southport road, the church is 1½ miles along the B5195.

Refreshments: None.

---

1. The first recorded church on the present site was in the early 15th century. The existing church of St Michael is 19th century, a pleasing black and white structure.

From the church, with the farm and outbuildings of Altcar Hall facing you, do not take either of the two tracks leading into the farmyard. Rather go left on the unsigned path by the old vicarage (a comparatively modern house). The wide grassed pathway is hedged on both sides. The end of the track exits onto the road through a white barrier, with bungalows to the left. Cross to the pavement on the far side of the road. Turn right along the road, passing Tatlock's Farm and then the village hall. In front of a hall is a map, showing the public rights of way in the parish of Altcar.

2. On reaching Clayton's Farm, turn right into Engine Lane. This starts between the thatched cottage on the right and Altcar Pumping Station on the left. At first, the stretch of the tarmac Engine Lane is hedged, but soon you are out in open hedgeless country. Turn the first left at a 'Private Road – no access' sign in the remains of what was once a hedge. Immediately after passing over a stream, the road

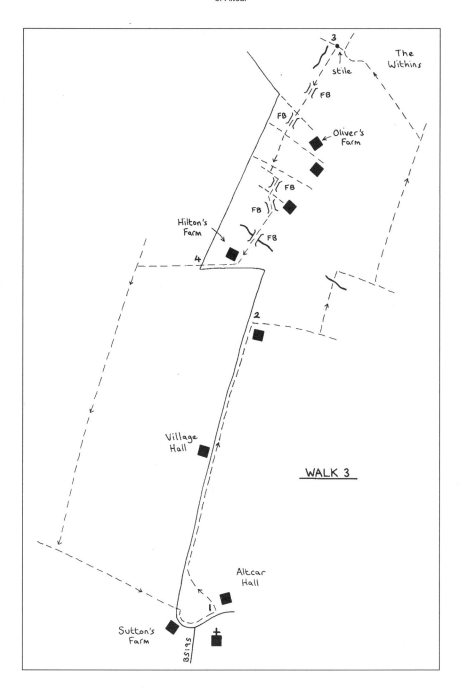

Thatched cottage, Altcar

turns sharply to the right. It runs parallel to telegraph poles on the right and a ditch on the left. As a dirt track goes ahead, turn left to continue on the tarmac road. (This is New Meadow Lane, but you would never know). Again, there is a ditch on the left, and one on the right that goes away at right angles after a while. This runs straight until it bends to the right over a wide drainage ditch.

3. Here turn left, before the white gate ahead. There are reeds on either side of the road. Over to the right is the area known as The Withins. This is the site where each February the hare coursing event called the Waterloo Cup has been run for over 100 years. This causes great controversy between the farming community who see it as part of their heritage and others who want the event banned, viewing it as unnecessary cruelty to hares. The straight road eventually becomes twistier. As a dirt track goes away to the right, there is a gate and footpath sign on the left. This is the start of Altcar Footpath no. 1.

Over the stile, walk across the field along the left edge of the stream. When the stream goes to the right, keep straight ahead to the other side of the field, aiming to the right end of the trees. Cross the foot-bridge into the next field. Follow the waymark straight ahead across this field, this time aiming for the gap in the hedge by a lone small tree. Cross the track leading to the farm, go down the slope and across the footbridge. Continue straight ahead, cross the raised farm track and walk to the left of the poles to another track. By the 5 mph sign at the farm entrance to the left, a footbridge brings you onto a track along the back of a barn. Cross the adjacent two tracks coming from the farm. Do not take the track to the right. To the right of a large tree, go straight ahead into the next field. Cross the footbridge to walk to the left of the hedge. Cross over the stream by means of a steel footbridge, hidden in a small clump of trees. Stay on the right side of the next field. After passing wooden palings to the right, the road is reached by the footpath sign adjacent to Hilton's Farm. The walk can be shortened here by turning left along the road back to the church. Otherwise, turn right along the road.

4. As the road bends sharply left, continue ahead along an unsigned tarmac path, which is actually called Livesley's Lane. You are now out on the sweeping vistas of Altcar Moss. On reaching a crossroads, with a dirt track going ahead, turn left, still on a tarmac lane (Middle Moss Lane). Soon after a large pylon on the left, turn left at the T-junction (this is Sutton's Lane). A 40 mph sign heralds the junction with the main road. Here turn right to go past Sutton's Farm and back to the church.

4. Birkdale Hills

*The sea, sand dunes and one of the most famous golf courses
in the country combine in this walk.*

Route: Sands Hotel – Round Hill – Royal Birkdale Golf Club –
Birkdale Sandhills.

Starting Point: Sands Hotel Ainsdale. Grid reference 302 128.

Distance: 5 miles.

Duration: 2 hours.

Map: Explorer 285.

By car: Car parking at Sands Hotel between the hotel and the lake.
This is situated by the roundabout adjacent to Pontins' holiday
complex, at the junction of Shore Road and the Woodvale to Southport
coastal road.

Refreshments: Sands Hotel.

---

1. From the Sands Hotel cross the Coast Road to walk up Shore Road.
On the corner are the Railway Cottages. The coast road was built
along the Cheshire Lines rail route when it closed in the 1950s.

The cottages housed railway workers who staffed Ainsdale Beach
station, situated on the coast road just north of the roundabout.
The station was opened in 1901, nearly 40 years after the opening of
the line itself. The original name 'Seaside' was changed to 'Ainsdale
Beach' in 1912. Both station and line closed in 1952.

From the roundabout, walk 200 metres up Shore Road. After passing a lane to the left, a blue Trans Pennine Trail sign, by a seat,
points you to the left. From the Birkdale Sandhills board, the
narrow path goes to the left. Look for the markers with a thin white
band. The way goes up and down through glades of trees, at one
point passing a well structure. After a marker at the top of a sand
dune, the path makes its way left through bracken and under-
growth. Reach the coast road by a marker with a white top.

Turn right along the cycle track. Within a few metres, locate a path,
which gradually works its way up from the cycle track. A white

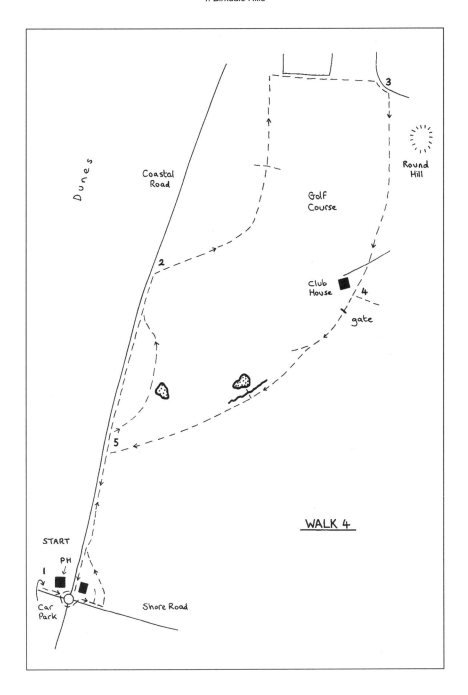

marker is visible along it. The path then runs parallel to the road, but far enough away from it to make walking quite pleasant. Eventually a large Sefton Coastal Footpath sign is reached. It indicates a right turn to Hillside, 1.5 km away. But carry straight on in the direction marked 'Birkdale Station 3 miles, Southport Station 4.5 miles'.

It is possible now to remain close to the coast road all the way to Birkdale, but there is, for some of the way, a more interesting route further from the road. The extra distance is small. Soon after the Coastal Footpath sign, a path branches to the right with a marker a few metres along it. Follow the path over the dunes. It passes a pond, which is over to the right. Then the path starts to work its way back towards the direction of the road. With the road in sight, stay to the right of the dune between path and road

2. The path now bends gradually right towards the fence of the golf course. (It is still possible to stay on the path parallel to the road, if required). After going over small dunes, drop down to a crossroads of paths. Keep straight on past the marker post ahead, then up to the right of bushes. You on are now on a wide plateau on many paths. Keep straight ahead towards the houses in the distance along a very wide grass track. After the Ainsdale and Birkdale Sandhills signpost, the track becomes a gravel one. At the end of the path, a footpath sign points to the left. Ignore it to turn right along Selworthy Road. At the end of the road, with Galworthy Road to the left, go straight ahead at the footpath sign on the path between a brick wall to the left and trees to the right.

3. Emerging in Selworthy Road, turn right at the footpath sign on the right, next to the gate with a 'Private' notice. Along the path, there are wooden palings to the left and trees bordering the golf course to the right. The path ends in a large public field. Keep on the track ahead along the bottom edge of the field. Over to the left is Round Hill. At the end of the field cross the access road, which has a fence along the far side. Walk along the other road, which is to its left. This takes you to the car park on the left of the Royal Birkdale golf club house with its 1930s art deco style.

Founded in 1889, this club moved to its present site eight years later. One of the premier golf clubs in Britain, in its turn it hosts the Open Championship.

Royal Birkdale Golf Club House

4. From the car park, go straight on, past a road coming in from the left, to a gate ahead. There is a 'Birkdale Sandhills' sign by the gate. The cement road quickly gives way to a wide dirt one. It narrows at a marker to become a sand track. At the next marker, stay on the main track ahead. This leads on to another marker in a small cluster of trees. Then bear right along the main path, not following any uphill to the left. After this keep on the path, gradually going up in a left-wards direction. Pass a Hillside direction sign, pointing in the direction from which you have just come. After passing to the left of a group of silver larch, do not take the track which goes off to the right, but bend up left and right to a marker, which cannot be sighted until near to it.

There is now a stretch of path through small shrubs and trees. When it divides, keep to the left of the small stream. (At the next path on the right, you may wish to divert the short distance to a beautiful small pond.) Carry on the left of the stream to pass a marker. The path continues through grass land, then through dunes to drop down onto the Coast Road.

5. Turn left from the Coastal Footpath sign, to follow the path near to the cycle track back to the Sands Hotel.

5. Cronton

*The ancient cross and hall are the focal points of this walk,
which includes the gentle incline of Pex Hill. Note: An
alternative Cronton walk appears as no. 18 in the author's
'East Lancashire Walks'.*

Route: Pex Hill – Cronton Hall – Lodge Lane – Upton Rocks – Pex Hill

Starting Point: Pex Hill Visitor Centre Grid reference: 502 888.

Distance: 4 or 6 miles.

Duration: 2 or 3 hours.

Map: Explorer 275.

By Car: Turn off the A5080 opposite to Widnes Sixth Form College.
Grid reference: 504 883. Coming from the Liverpool direction, after
passing through the village, look out for Cronton Nurseries on the left.
Then turn sharp left on the next bend, after the house. Follow the road,
through the green railings, to the Visitor Centre at the top of the hill.

Refreshments: Unicorn Inn at the village crossroads.

---

1. From the car park in front of the Visitor Centre, go through the gate
onto the picnic area. Ignoring the path going sharp right, take the
right-hand one of the two, descending downhill. There are extensive views on the right over the plain towards the Mersey. The railings around the old quarry are next on the right. At the T-junction,
turn right along the wide path, which takes you along the other side
of the quarry. Then, with a path descending steps to the right, turn
left down Mill Lane. This sunken track has been in use for many
centuries. Coming to the barrier at the bottom of the track, carry
straight on along the tarmac road. There are houses on the right and
fields to the left.

2. At the T-junction, turn right. On your left is the Holy Family Catholic Church, next to its school. On the right corner is what looks like a
vintage petrol pump. The road runs through the centre of the village. You will come to Cronton Hall on the right-hand side of the
road. This is surrounded by houses and cottages dating from the 17th

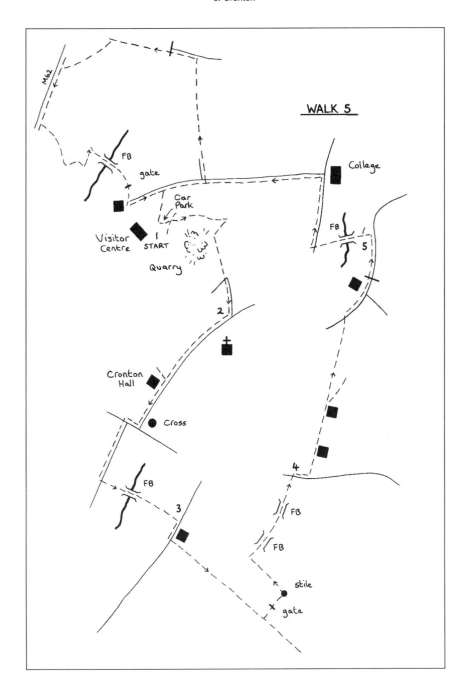

WALK 5

century. Sunnyside Farm, to the right of the Hall, is from a century earlier. In between the farm and the Hall runs a footpath to Rainhill. The Hall itself is early 18th century.

At the junction with Hall Lane, notice the remains of the ancient cross of the left-hand corner. Most of these wayside crosses were resting places for funeral corteges, as the coffin was born to the nearest church. In those days, this could be miles away. Turn right up Hall Lane and immediately left into Penny Lane. On the left corner is the aptly named Stone Cross Farm. On the right is Town End Farm. The countryside soon opens up before you, as you walk along Penny Lane. Just before reaching Tue Lane, there is a footpath sign on the left, indicating 'Cronton Road $^1/_3$ mile.' The path takes you across the centre of the field, towards a footbridge over a stream.

Go straight on across the middle of the next field, aiming to the right of the tree ahead. Here the path stays to the right of a ditch. When the ditch ends, continue straight ahead. The path, as it gets near to the road, runs to the right of a ditch and hedge.

3. Before turning right along Cronton Road, notice the outline of Runcorn Bridge on the horizon. After turning right, the first house on the left is The Croft. Follow the footpath sign, on the far side of the house, indicating 'Stockwell Road'. This is Lodge Lane, a wide farm track. Pass the farm on the right at Caxton Lodge. Passing a footpath sign pointing to the left, keeping going until reaching another footpath sign. Here turn left along the farm track, which takes you to a field gate. Go through the gap to the left of the gate. Proceed, with the hedge on your left. Before reaching the other side of the field, you will come to a footbridge on your left.

Cross the stream, to follow the path across the field. At the signpost indicating 'Chapel Lane $^1/_3$ mile', turn right down the track by the ditch. Then go on across the field to cross a bridge, adjacent to a hedge. Now stay on the right-hand side of the ditch. As this swings away to the left, go on to the tree ahead. Do not take the wide track going off to the left, but cross the footbridge to the right of the tree. Stay to the right of the ditch, with the occasional tree along the way. As the ditch ends, go straight across the field towards the road. Go up the steps onto Chapel Lane.

4. Cross the road and turn right. Go round the bend, passing the

Cronton Hall

houses on the left. Then look for a footpath sign and gate in the hedge. Through the gate, go straight on, passing the left of the wooden shed and nursery grounds. Resist the temptation to carry on through the wide gap into the next field. Instead, go left into the adjacent field to turn immediately right along the hedge and ditch side. This is a long path, which eventually swings left away from the ditch to go round the edge of a copse onto Sandy Lane.

Turn right to the T-junction. On the left, at the time of writing, is a barn and derelict cottage. Go left along Old Upton Lane. Go between the bollards across the road, then continue through the housing estate.

5. As the road bends sharply to the right, on the left is a footpath, which soon joins another one coming in from the right. The cross field path comes to a footbridge, soon after running a short distance to the right of a ditch and hedge. Over the bridge, cross the field to join Cronton road. Turn right. Then on the bend turn left, opposite Wigan Sixth Form College. Walk up the road on which you travelled when arriving to get back to the Visitor Centre.

It is possible to extend the walk for an extra distance at this point. Walk back through the main entrance to the car park. Turn left along the tarmac road, opposite to the house named Shalimar. Walk on between the reservoir fences. On reaching houses ahead, with the notice, 'Private Residences' turn right along a wide grass track, with woodland to the left and the reservoir bank on the right. At the gate, the M62 can be seen in the distance.

Through the gate, bear left, following the downhill path to the right of the hedge. Over the footbridge, go across the middle of the field. The path then bears left along the edge of the field, with railings on the right. After passing a lone tree, immediately after the telegraph pole, turn right along the cart track. There is a stream on the left and more railings on the right. Next, turn left along a wide tarmac track. This swings to the right, then bends its way towards the M62. At the T-junction, opposite to the motorway, turn right towards the masts ahead. As a dirt track runs straight ahead, turn sharp right along a wide tarmac road.

At the barriers, turn right along the road and cycle track. This stretch is no long open to traffic. Pass through the next set of barriers. After the first house on the right, turn right at the footpath sign indicating 'Pex Hill'. The path goes uphill, staying on the left side of the field. At the top corner of the field, continue straight on uphill. There are trees on the left and houses to the right. After passing 'The Cottage' on the right, the path widens for a short distance. At the T-junction, turn right back to the Visitor Centre.

6. Croxteth

A old hall, streams, fields and woods on the edge of urban Liverpool combine to make this walk a delight.

Route: West Derby parish church – Stand Hall Farm – Cocked Hat Wood – Croxteth Hall West Derby church.

Starting Point: West Derby church, Town Row, West Derby Village. Grid reference 398 934.

Distance: 5 miles.

Duration: 2 hours, excluding visiting the Hall and other attractions.

Map: Explorer 275.

By Car: The church and starting point is at the end of Mill Lane, off Queens Drive (A5058).

Refreshments: At start/finish point there is plenty of choice. Three pubs – The Lord Sefton, West Derby and Horse & Jockey – plus an off-licence and fish and chip shop. At Croxteth Hall, refreshments are also available during the season.

---

1. The Gothic style Village cross is mid-19th century. A figure of Christ surmounts the five shafts.

The small cottage to west of cross is the Court House dating from 1662. The Hare and Hounds dates from the early 19th century.

Walk through the gates, whose pillars are surmounted by lions with flags. The lodge is on the right and the church to the left. St Mary's Church was built between 1853 and 1856 at the instigation of Lord Sefton. The architect was George Gilbert Scott, father of Giles of Liverpool Anglican Cathedral fame. It replaced the church of 1793. Continue along the wide path with open land on either side until reaching a crossroads, just after a 'sleeping policeman'. Follow the sign that points straight ahead to the farm and gardens. After another sleeping policeman, arrive at Croxteth Lodge, going through the white gates. To the left is a toilet block and car park. Head for the underpass that passes below Croxteth Hall Lane. Soon after the miniature railway station on the left and before reaching the hall ahead, turn left at the sign to Colt Paddock and Games Field.

Follow the path, which has a wire fence on the right. Ignore a path to the left. On the same side after this is a sculptured tree trunk. As the path swings right to a tarmac path, ignore another path on the left. At the tarmac, the oblong Statue Pond is on the right. But turn left along the path, next going over a stone walled bridge, then through wooden gates. Turn along the dirt path to the left through the woods, following it to the right by a post with a green arrow and No. 2. The wide path travels through the woodland, later with a pond and ducks in the rhododendrons on the right. The path swings right at the next green arrow, straight across the tarmac path (another arrow).

2. Then it makes its way through woodlands, with fields to be seen to the right. Reaching the River Alt, follow the arrow to the right, then immediately turn left across the bridge, left and quickly right again. With a stream on the right and woods to the left, walk up the stone path. This continues onto a wider track (ignoring all paths to the right). At the tarmac service road, turn right. This way goes through woods, with a wire fence on the left. At the sign post, follow ahead in the direct of the Riding Centre (Stand Farm). (To shorten the walk at this stage, simply follow the sign pointing to 'Hall Farm and Gardens' to the right.)

Continue, ignoring the next path to the right. Eventually the path does a short bend left and right, although walkers have obviously straightened the bend out by making a path straight ahead. Now out in open land, come to another signpost. Follow the sign to the left, announcing 'Cocked Hat Wood'. The tarmac road passes to the left of Stand House Farm, a cottage and the Kennels. After a wooden shed on the left is a pedestrian entrance to the park. But go ahead, between the metal posts, on the stone track through more woodland. (An almost immediate turn right towards a field gate and left turn before reaching it, brings you onto a dirt track, which runs parallel with the stone one.)

3. With houses immediately in front, follow the track to the right, keeping the houses to the left. At the end of the buildings, pass a path on the left and a pond. Fields and a farm are now visible to the

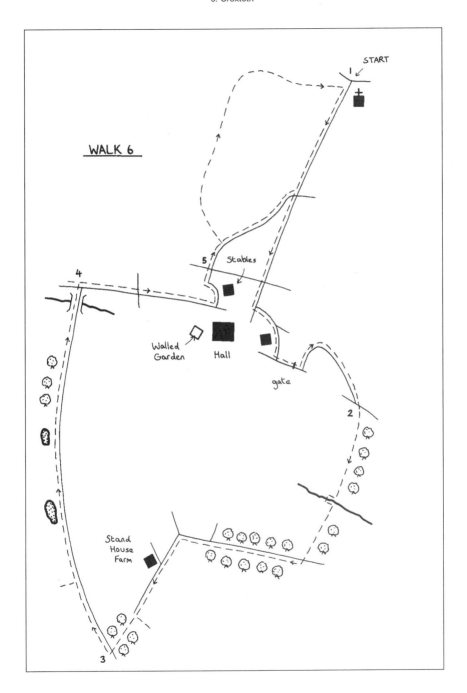

WALK 6

START

Stables

Walled Garden

Hall

gate

Stand House Farm

left. The path soon bends to the right, passing another pond and private notices on the left. The winding path has houses again to the left, glimpst through the woodland. Eventually, there is a barbed wired fence on the right and wooden one on the left. Look right across the fields to see Stand House Farm in the distance. Pass through a gate to the path junction at Knowsley Drive Gate.

4. Turn right onto the tarmac path and over the bridge. There is a stream to the right and field railings to the left. Croxteth Hall can be seen ahead. At a crossroads, follow the path ahead, through open land of trees and rhododendrons to the Hall. Here signposts direct to the Hall entrance, farm, and gardens.

The remains of the first hall, which was erected towards the end of

the 16th century, can be seen at the rear of the present building. When the Molyneux family decided to move permanently from their other home in Sefton, the grand Queen Anne wing was erected 1702-14 and the grounds laid out. In the 19th century, the Home Farm and walled garden were added. A 1952 fire destroyed some rooms in the wing. When the 7th Earl died in 1972, his widow gave the hall and estate to the Council. Although part of the estate is now built over, the rest plus the hall are open to the public.

Croxteth Hall: The Queen Anne Wing (by permission of Croxteth Hall and Country Park)

Leave by the sign to Croxteth Hall Lane. This passes over a sleeping policeman, bends to the left by the farm to a big signpost. Turn right along the road.

5. At Croxteth Hall Lane, cross over the road to the Lodge. Follow the path to its left. Here is a choice of ways. The shortest is to go ahead on the wide path to the signpost, then turn left along the path used at the start of the walk heading toward the church. The alternative is soon to turn left on a worn path across the field towards houses in the distance. Before reaching the houses, follow the path to the right, which stays close to the edging woodland. Follow this, passing a path that goes off to the right and walk through a small copse. Stay by the wood edge as it passes to the left of a pond. After some time, the path emerges, through trees, between railings to the right and the lodge to the left. Turn left back the few metres to the starting point.

7. Halewood

The country park is based on the old railway line. The walk then meanders around open fields.

Route: Halewood Country Park – Loop Line – Foxhill House – Halewood Village.

Starting Point: Okell Drive Visitor Centre, Halewood. Grid reference: 440 863.

Distance: 5 miles.

Duration: 2 hours.

Map: Explorer 275.

Train: Halewood Station is on the Merseyrail Liverpool – Hunts Cross line. From the station pick up the walk at point no. 6.

By Car: From the junction of the M62 and M57 take the road signposted to Huyton. At the traffic lights turn left into Whitefield Lane, then left again into Netherley Road. then take first right in Green's Bridge Road. Follow this until Halewood Village is reached. Turn right along Church Lane, passing the Eagle and Child and the parish church. At the roundabout, turn left into Okell Drive. After the road bends right, the Visitor Centre for Halewood Country Park is on the left.

Refreshments: Eagle and Child, Church Road.

---

1. From in front of the Visitor centre, go left the short distance to reach the archway towering over the small pyramid. Follow the sign to the right directing toward Ducky Pond and cycleway. This takes you through woodland. Go straight on at the cross paths to reach another signpost. Go to the left in the Ducky Pond direction. The wide track makes its way first through more woodland, but open ground is soon visible to the right. The track curves on, crossing a dry stream bed. Avoid all paths going off to the left. At the pond, turn right at the T-junction. (The right turn, a few metres before this, only cuts off a short distance.) Stay on this main track, ignoring dirt paths going off to the left as the track bends to the right. Pass through an avenue of trees. On reaching another T-junction, turn

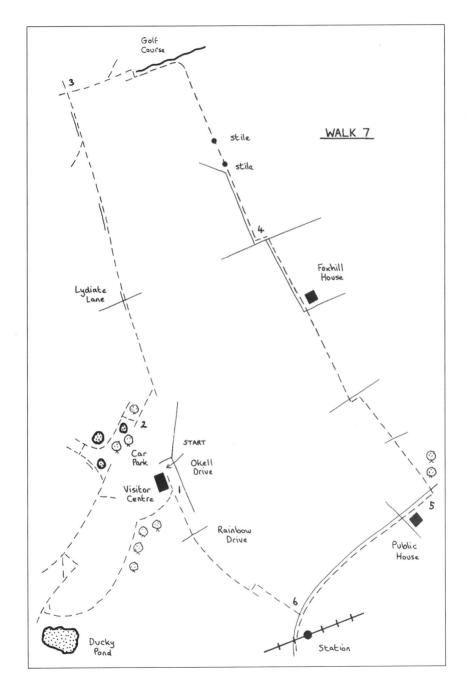

Golf Course

3

stile

stile

WALK 7

4

Foxhill House

Lydiate Lane

2

START

Car Park

Okell Drive

Visitor Centre

1

Rainbow Drive

5

Public House

6

Ducky Pond

Station

left the few metres to the old Liverpool loop line rail track. This is now part of the Southport to Hull Trans-Pennine Trail.

Turn right onto this very wide avenue, remembering to keep an eye open for cyclists. There are trees on either side. Coming to a signpost, keep on in the direction of Gateacre. You will soon come to a left turn off the track. Follow this up an incline, passing a pond on the right. Pass over a level bridge. At a split in the paths go right and then quickly right again at the T-junction. You will go past another pond down to the left as the path bend left and then right again past railings.

Halewood Triangle

Walk between the houses, then past a school field to the left and the stream on the right, through the woodland. At the third and final pond, turn right.

2. Arriving back by the signpost at the main track, turn left in the direction of Gateacre again. Carry on over the crossroad of paths. There is woodland on the right and at first open land to the left followed by houses. After a length of now redundant railings in the wood to the right, pass the signpost pointing to Lydiate Lane and go over the bridge.

From here, the track gradually ascends along the embankment. This gives extensive views over to the right. After the unsightly breeze-block bridge, carry on. Immediately after a track coming in from the left, go over another bridge.

3. A hundred metres beyond this on the right are black painted steps, leading down from the embankment. At the bottom of the steps, turn right along the path coming from under the railway bridge.

There is a wire fence on the right. Go through the nature area to take this first turn to the right. This takes you between small trees on the left and a fence to the right. At the next T-junction turn right down to the stream Above you to the right is a signpost pointing left to Gerrards Lane, three-quarters of a mile away. Follow the right bank of Gerrards Brook. There is a large pipe running just above it. Go over a side stream at a clump of trees. The path continues to run between the fence of the water treatment plant and the brook. Go under a large pipe. The buildings of the water treatment plant can now be seen on the right. On the other side of the stream are the grounds of Lee Park Golf Course. At the footpath sign pointing right to Gerrards Lane, now half a mile away, turn right along the side of the large field. The stream continues away to the left. In the corner of the field is a gate, which leads into a grass path between high hedges. This gets wider, with large trees appearing by the path. At the next gate and footpath sign pointing back to Halewood Road, turn left up the road (North End Lane).

4. At the T-junction, go left for a short distance along Gerrards Lane. Go right into Foxhill Lane to reach Foxhill House on the corner. Go straight ahead along the track through the middle of the large field opposite. On reaching the footpath sign on Cartbridge Lane, cross to the pavement on the other side of the road. Go left to another footpath sign. Here turn right over the stream by the gate. The path takes you through the middle of a housing estate, crossing an estate road en route. The path ends in woodland.

5. Turn right along a wider path by the sign directing to Halewood Village. The path merges into Court Avenue, with houses on both sides. At Church Road, turn left by the Eagle and Child pub, then immediately right into Hollies Road. After passing the Community Centre and 9th Knowsley Scouts Headquarters, cross the entrance to Crantock Close.

6. Just after Plantation Primary School and before Halewood Station, turn right along the path between the embankment and the school field. At the chicane, go left up onto the embankment. Turn right along the main track. Ignoring all paths to the left, pass by a seat, go through another chicane, walk across Rainbow Drive. Stay on the path to arrive pack at the Visitor Centre and car park.

8. Hightown to Freshfield Linear Walk

A rifle range, an asparagus field and red squirrels feature on a walk never far from the coast.

Route: Hightown – Alt Bridge – Cabin Hill – Wicks Wood – Freshfield.

Starting Point: Hightown Station or Alt Centre. Grid reference: 300 037 or 297 037.

Distance: 5 miles.

Duration: 3 hours.

Map: Explorer 285.

By Train: Merseyrail Northern Line to Southport.

By Car: At the roundabout in the village centre turn right. Park the car just before the 'No through road' sign. The Alt Centre is on the left, 30 metres further on.

Refreshments: Shops at Hightown and Freshfield. An ice cream van, which sells drinks as well, operates during the summer months by the red squirrel reserve towards the end of the walk.

---

*1A.***From Hightown Station.** On the village side of the station, turn immediately right along a tarmac road with a 'Keep Out' sign. This applies only to vehicular traffic. The road runs parallel to the railway. It passes under the road overpass. At this point, there is a barrier to stop vehicles going through. Further along the road are notices that you are nearing the Rifle Range. Continue and, just to the right of the entrance, you will see a footpath sign pointing along the side of the railway towards Formby.

*1B.***From the Alt Centre:** with the Centre on the left and the boatyard on the right, turn right along the tarmac road. The River Alt is now on your left-hand side. After the boatyards, there are houses on the right.

As the houses come to an end, you are faced by a barrier, warning

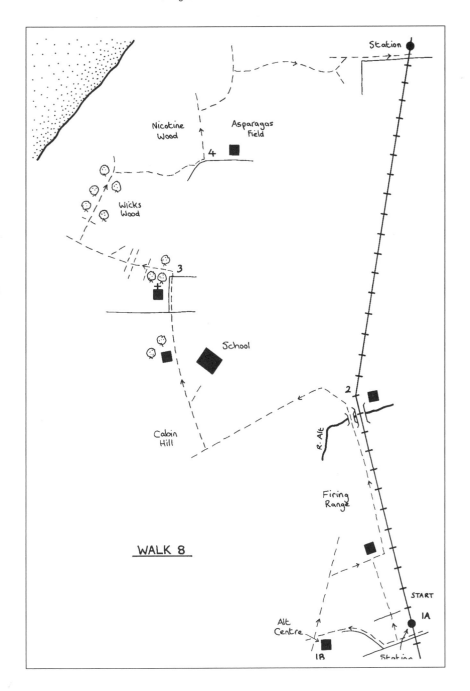

Station

Nicotine
Wood

Asparagas
Field

4

Wicks
Wood

3

School

Cabin
Hill

2

R. Alt

Firing
Range

WALK 8

START

1A

Alt
Centre

1B

Station

'Firing range keep out'. Here turn right at the Sefton Coastal Footpath sign. The narrow path runs along the back of the houses, with a fence separating it from the Rifle Range grounds on the left. At the end of the path, the entrance to the Range is on the left. Between it and the railway is a footpath sign to Formby.

This is the meeting point of routes 1A and 1B. The stone path runs between the perimeter of the rifle range and the railway for the next mile.

On the right can be seen the sidings which linked the Lancashire and Yorkshire Railway to the range. The station, called Hightown Rifle Station, opened in 1862. Ammunition was carried from the station to the range by means of a tramway. The station eventually closed in 1921. The range itself came into operation in 1860, the first shot being fired by the Earl of Sefton on 28 July of that year. The author has mixed memories of trying to fire a rifle here for the first time during National Service in 1956. Today the range is used mainly by the Territorial Army.

After a stone wall on the right, the path dips below the level of the railway. The path itself dates from 1939, when, on the outbreak of war, all public rights of way across the range were closed and exchanged for the present one. On the left are now two rows of fencing to prevent intruders. Passing by a bungalow at the level crossing, the path continues straight on, with shrub land to the left. After going over a bridge over a stream, the path begins to bend after passing a seat on the right. The fence on the right is now further away from the path. After bushes and railings on the right, the path crosses over the River Alt by means of a bridge. The large derelict building on the other side of the railway was the Power House, which from 1904-48 produced power for the trains after the electrification of the track. The bridge is at the lowest point on the River Alt, whose source is in Huyton Meadows, 18 miles away.

Visible to the left, in the trees, is Alt Grange and Farm. This was lived in by the Blundell family in the 13th century and later used by the monks from Stanlow Abbey, before they moved to Whalley Abbey in 1296. In the 18th century, the Grange was by the mouth of the river, as it entered the sea. This is a sign of how far the sea has retreated since then.

2. From the bridge, the path swings to the left away from the railway, with a stream to the right. At the crossroad of paths, turn left along the narrow fenced track. On the right are open fields and a ditch. The left is still the perimeter of the Firing Range. After passing a barrier and coastal path sign, there are small trees on the right-hand side. At a copse, where the path continues straight on towards the beach, turn right along the wide cart track. After passing by woodland, the track goes on through open ground.

On the left is Cabin Hill, which was the name of a huge sand dune, which used to act a landmark for shipping out in the bay. The sand was removed in the middle of the 20th century. The area is now a reserve managed by English Nature. In it are found sand lizards and Natterjack toads as well as a variety of rare plants.

As the main track swings to the right, carry straight on along the wide grass track. On the right are the large grounds of Range High School. Go past a bungalow in the woodland, then on into the open along the stone path, ignoring a stile on the left. Back in woodland, on the right are the fences of houses. At the crossroad of paths, follow the Coastal Path sign ahead, along the tarmac road. At the next crossroads, with Shorrocks Hill Country Club and Lifeboat Road on the left, continue ahead. On the left is St Luke's Church. The church was built in the middle of the 19th century by the Formby family. Many of them are buried in the churchyard, where also can be found a market cross and stocks.

3. At the point that St Luke's Church Road bends sharply right, turn left through the woods. Keep straight ahead until the trees come to an end. Descend the wooden steps to come to a cross road of paths. Keep straight on up the steps at the other side of the small valley. The clearly marked path crosses over two other path intersections, until joining with another path coming in from the right. Over to the right is Wicks Wood. Take any of the grass paths leading towards it or, alternatively, stay on the main path until reaching the sign pointing to the right. After passing a wooden seat, you will arrive at the Formby Point sign at the entrance to the wood, with a seat to the right. Pass the coastal path sign, proceeding straight through the wood. Coming out into the open, the path soon passes through more woodland ahead. After the path has swung to the right, a triangle is reached. Do not follow the Coastal Path sign, but turn right along the wide path. Ignore paths to the right, as it passes through more woodland.

4. As the path reaches a tarmac road, by the horseshoe sign, turn sharp left. On the right are Sandfield Farm and an asparagus field – one of the few remaining in the area. In the 1930s, asparagus was grown for use on the passenger liners that sailed from Liverpool. At the fork of paths, bear right towards Nicotine Wood. The path runs through the wood, then open land. Just before the main track goes uphill, turn right at the Woodland Walk sign. This bears left, then right, through the narrow strip of woodland. After passing the board walk to the picnic site on the right, go left at the fork of paths. This takes you onto a short uphill stretch to a wide concrete road. On the right is the red squirrel reserve area. The post-war invasion of grey squirrels has left very few colonies of the red variety. One of the nearest to this is, somewhat surprisingly, in the grounds of Southport Crematorium on Southport Road. On the other side of the road are public toilets. Turn right along the concrete road past the National Trust car park entrance. Carry straight on down Victoria Road, with its large houses, to arrive at Freshfield Station.

9. Hoylake – West Kirby

From the heights of Caldy Hill to the shore of the Dee Estuary, this walk is always full of interest and variety.

Route: Hoylake Station – Gilroy Nature Park – Grange Hill – Caldy Hill – Marine Lake – Red Rocks – Hoylake Station.

Starting Point: Hoylake Merseyrail Station. Grid reference: 217 888.

Distance: 6 miles.

Duration: 3 hours.

Map: Explorer 266.

By Train: Hoylake Station is on the Merseyrail Wirral Line.

By Car: From the roundabout at the junction of Market Street (A553) and Meols Drive (A540), turn into Station Road.

Refreshments: Moby Dick pub, West Kirby.

1. Turn left from the station along Carr Lane. The club house of Hoylake golf course can be seen on the right. Go right into Newhall Lane. After the industrial units on both sides, it is a surprise to reach the adjacent working farm on the right. At this point, the wide tarmac road narrows. After a field on the left, there is a sign warning of flying balls, as the lane crosses the golf course. There are pylons going away to the left. You are soon walking, with fields to the left and the course on the right. The lane swings right, then left again to a straight stretch. In the distance on the hill ahead can be seen the War Memorial and Mariners Beacon you will be passing later in the walk. After passing a footbridge to the left and over the small River Birket, the lane narrows and the terrain becomes a little wilder.

After you pass a small coppice, a board on the right announces arrival at Gilroy Nature Park. Since the board only caters for people walking in the opposite direction, you have to look on the other side of it for the notices. If time allows, a visit to the park will uncover ponds, paths and seats. From the boards, continue along the main path to reach Gilroy Road at a footpath sign. After turning right, you come to a small tree-embellished village green. To its right is Coronation Buildings, which contains the Post Office amongst other shops.

2. Turn left up Greenbank Road and first right into Somerset Road. At the end, this narrows into a tarmac footpath, which bends right and then left, with houses on the right and a children's playground on the left. At the left turn, leave the path to walk along the left edge of the fence on the grass. As the fence ends, continue across the field to reach a wide cross path on the edge of the cemetery.

Turn right along the path to exit through the cemetery gates. Just after the Lang Lane road sign, with Gresford Avenue going off to the right, turn left on the narrow footpath uphill through the heather. After a few metres, at the fork in the path, keep to the right. This path continues its undulating way gradually uphill. The War Memorial looms ahead. From the Memorial and the surrounding land, there are expansive views over the Dee Estuary. Go left along the ridge path away from the Memorial. After passing the trig point, the path narrows, bearing to the right by palings and trees. It continues high above the road to come out on Old Grange Road. Go left, passing the Hoylake Sea Cadets HQ on the right and a footpath sign on the left. At the roundabout, with Black Horse Hill road on the left, continue ahead along Column Road, passing Village Road, towards the Mariners' Beacon, which is difficult to miss.

The Mariners' Beacon

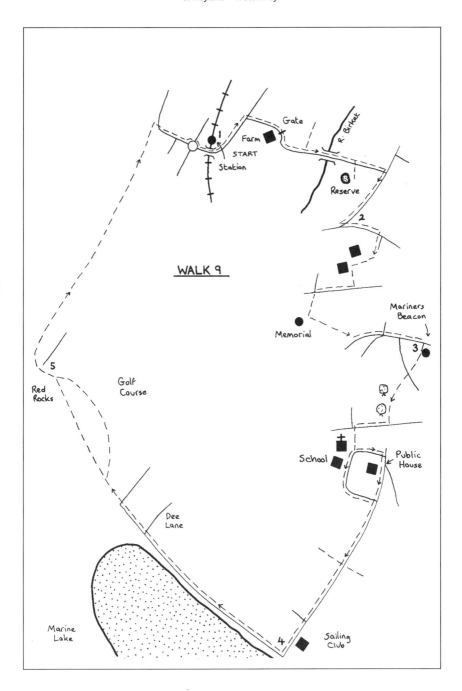

WALK 9

3. As from the War Memorial, the views from this point on Caldy Hill are some of the best in the area. A footpath sign points towards Echo Lane. Follow this down the steps cut in the rock and on through the trees. At the bottom, cross the road to the footpath sign following a wide path down the hill. It at first runs between stone walls and fences. Later there is woodland on the right.

At the road, turn right downhill between the fields. At St Bridget's church, turn left along the walled path. The road widens on reaching St Bridget's school. At the T-junction, there is a choice of ways:

Longer route:

Turn left along St Bridgets Lane, then right downhill through West Kirby village. At the Moby Dick pub, turn right down Sandy Lane.

Shorter route:

Turn right down Ludlow Drive to meet Sandy Lane at the T-junction.

Further along Sandy Lane, pass over the bridge, under which runs the Wirral Way. The sea is now in sight at the end of the road.

4. After passing West Kirby Sailing Club on the left, turn right along the promenade, South Parade. On the left is the Marine Lake. Especially at week ends, there is always busy mixture of boats and surf boards. Soon after the Sailing Centre, the promenade ends.

The walk across the sands from West Kirby to Hilbre Island Local Nature Reserve is deservedly popular, but it will add some hours to the walk and you must be sure of the tide times. Information is posted at the end of the promenade, and for further information about arranging visits to Hilbre, please see page 135

The road, Riversdale, goes off at right angles. Walk ahead, down the steps, onto the sand below. When the houses to the right end, there are some boulders to prevent vehicular traffic. Either go on the sand path ahead or go up the board walk to the right to follow the path adjacent to the Royal Liverpool golf course, higher up in the dunes. The lower path continues until reaching Red Rocks. The higher path reaches the same destination, with the added excitement of passing through reed beds and marsh land in the later stages. This is the Red Rocks Nature Reserve. The red rocks at Hilbre Point are a curious collection of odd-shaped sandstone. Out in the estuary can be seen Hilbre and Little Hilbre Islands.

5. From the Point cross the slipway at Stanley Road to follow round the headland and the curve of the bay. Exit from the beach at the third opening, having passed a wide and then a small one beforehand.

The landmark is a small stone battlemented turret on the seafront, adjacent to North Parade and The King's Gap. This is so called because William of Orange made his way along here to the shore to set sail for the Battle of the Boyne in Ireland. The battlemented theme continues with the walls of Kings Court. Over to the left can be seen an old lighthouse. Pass Stanley Road, then the parish church of St Hildeburgh and the Scientology Church, as you make for the roundabout. Just beyond Hoylake Chapel is the rail station.

10. Kirkby: 1

Hardly out of sight of the town of Kirkby, this country walk includes the old coach road to Knowsley Hall and passes by ancient Mossborough Hall.

Route: Coach Road – Woodside Farm – Harrison's Wood – Mossborough Hall – New Cut Lane – Gore's Farm.

Starting Point: Small lay-by with SOS telephone, just before the Lodge. Grid reference: 457 970.

Distance: 4½ or 5 miles.

Duration: 2 to 3 hours.

Map: Explorer 275.

By Car: east of Kirkby on the A580 East Lancashire Road.

Refreshments: None.

---

1. From the lay-by walk to the entrance gates of the lodge by the footpath sign. Do not be put off by the notice on the gates stating 'Private Road – authorised users only'. This only applies to vehicular traffic. Go through the turnstile. Walk along the wide tree lined Coach Road, with fields on either side.

This road has been here at least since the 17ᵗʰ century. Lord Derby, based at Knowsley Hall, owns much of the land for many miles around. It is worked by tenant farmers. The road starts in Bickerstaffe, two miles away. It was bisected by the building of the East Lancs road. This resulted in the building of two new lodges on either side of that road.

After passing a large pylon in a field on the left, a footpath sign, with four indicators, will be seen. Take the stile on the right, opposite to the lane going off to the left. The word 'Footpath' is written on the stile in yellow letters. With the hedge to the left, walk along the wide farm track. After passing Emma Wood, which is to the right, you come to Woodside Farm. Continue on the track as it swings sharply to the right through the farm outbuildings. In front of the farm house

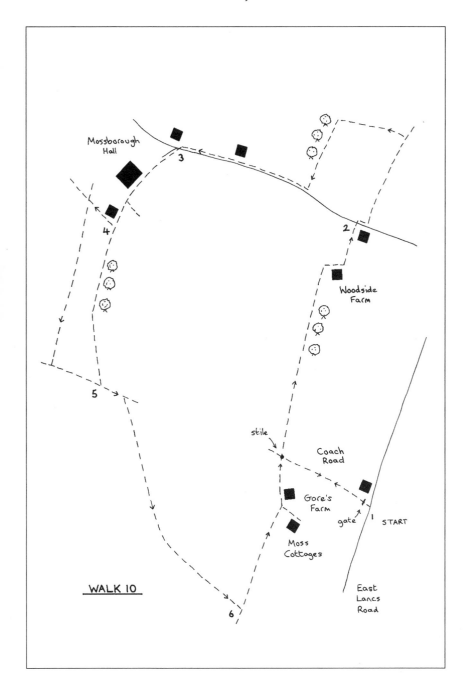

Mossborough Hall

3

4

2

Woodside Farm

5

stile

Coach Road

Gore's Farm

gate   1   START

Moss Cottages

WALK 10

6

East Lancs Road

on the right, the track veers to the left. Now hedged, the track arrives at Blind Foot Road (B5203). There is a house on the corner, by a footpath sign.

2. Turn right along the pavement, then cross the road to a footpath sign. Walk along the left side of the stream, which is in a deep tree lined gully. At the end of the field, by a telegraph pole, one path sign points from the way that you have just come and another straight on. A separate one points to the left. This is the one to follow. The way is along the right-hand side of the intermittent hedge. On reaching Harrison's Wood, you are discouraged from going ahead by a sign stating 'Strictly Private – No Footpath'. The way is now along the farm track, which goes to the left, along the edge of the wood. At the end of the wood, it continues across the open field to reach the B5203 again, opposite to Blind Foot Farm. Turn right, along the road. After a few footsteps, a pavement begins. Stay on this, passing Blind Foot Cottage en route, until reaching the old Mossborough cottages at the junction with Mossborough Hall Lane.

3. Go left down the hedged lane to arrive at Mossborough Hall, which is on the right.

The only remains of the original 14th-century hall to be seen are the parts of the moat, which survived filling in operations over the centuries. The crest of the Molyneux (Sefton) family is displayed on the front wall. One of the interior rooms has wooden carved panels dating from 1626, which were rescued from refurbishment at Knowsley Hall in the 1950s.

From the Hall, remain on the same track.

4. Coming to a bungalow on the right, there is a choice of routes.

The shorter one is to keep straight one, passing the copse, which is to the left. The path then turns 90% to the left, passing some houses. At the T-junction, just after a bungalow, rejoin the longer route.

For the longer route, turn right at the footpath sign by the bungalow. The track has a barbed wire fence on its right. There is sometimes a gate across it at one point. At the cross road of tracks, turn left. This wide track takes you across the middle of a huge open field. At the T-junction, turn left. You are now back on the Coach

May 1950: Mossborough Hall

Road. On the left are the stumps of ancient trees, brought to the surface by the constant ploughing of the fields. After passing the entrance to Blind Foot Farm, which is on the right, the junction with Mossborough Hall Lane is reached, just after some derelict brick buildings on the left. This is the junction with the shorter route.

5. Proceed straight ahead, still on the Coach Road. It is now flanked by trees. At the sign pointing back to Bickerstaffe and on to the East Lancs Road, turn right. The dirt track takes you between a hedge on the left and trees alongside a stream on the right. The path joins a wide stone track coming in from the right at a wooden post marked 'Footpath'. The wide track goes as straight as an arrow. The only building to pass is a lone cottage and outbuilding. Unwelcome visitors are deterred by a notice announcing the presence of a dog and the command to visitors by car to blow the horn and wait. After the cottage, the ground to the left drops away. On the right is a large pylon, which is an indicator that the end of this long stretch of New Cut Lane is not far away.

6. At the junction, follow the sign pointing left to the Coach Road. This pleasant winding raised tarmac road has the only two trees to be seen for some distance. On the right are the white Moss Cottages. Soon after passing the lane to these on the right, the road bends to the left in front of Gore's Farm. The wooden shed, after the outbuildings, must have the greatest lean of any similar one in the world. The now hedged track passes the pylon in the field on the right to arrive at the junction with the Coach Road. Turn right down the lane, which you came up at the start of the walk, to arrive back at the lodge gates.

11. Kirkby: 2

An inner town greenway walk, never far from Kirkby Brook.

Route: St Chad's Church – St Chad's Park – Mill Pond – Valley Park – St Chad's Church.

Starting Point: St Chad's Church, Old Hall Road. Grid reference: 408 989.

Distance: 3 miles.

Duration: 1 hour or so.

Map: Explorer 275.

By Car: From junction 6 on the M57, drive north along Valley Road (passing Kirkby Stadium). At the roundabout turn left into Kirkby Road, then right into Old Hall Lane.

By Train: Kirkby Station is the Merseyrail terminus from Liverpool on the Northern Line. From the station walk down Kirkby Row, turning left into Old Hall Lane immediately after James Holt Avenue on the right.

Refreshments: None.

---

1. St Chad's was the parish church of the old Kirkby village, before it expanded into a town in the 1950s. From the church, cross the road to go through the entrance to St Chad's Park. Having passed the lodge on the right, which is just inside the entrance, stay on the path that runs along the right side of the park. Half way round, by another entrance, will be found the Weeping Stone.

This ancient stone was originally known as Park Brow Cross, because of its location at Park Brow, some half mile south west of the present site. It was a stopping place for local Catholics, taking coffins to St Swithin's church, Gillmoss for burial – hence its name. It was restored by Lord Sefton in 1880.

Continue round the perimeter of the park. Ignoring paths to the left, exit on to Hall Lane. Turn left, crossing Old Hall Lane. Immediately beyond the Centre 63 Youth Centre and opposite to Kirkby Baths, turn left along a tarmac path. This takes you between Centre 63 on

The ancient Weeping Stone

the left and the playing field of Kirkby C of E Primary School to the right. After passing through the barrier, proceed straight ahead, not taking the path to the left. You are now crossing open grassland, with Kirkby Brook over to the left in the distance. As the path makes it way towards the rail bridge ahead, notice the three emblems spaced out on the right at intervals.

The first is entitled 'A fertile land', the second 'An industrious people' and finally 'A wealth of talent, Kirkby'. Between the second and third, it is possible to extend the walk a little by following the wide cut grass path in a semicircle.

2. Go under the rail bridge, with the brook on the left, through the barrier to cross Mill Lane to the right of Mill Bridge. Follow the path up in the direction of the houses, but then take the one that goes left down towards the pond. Cross the bridge over the brook, then turn immediately right over the wooden bridge. Walk along the path between the pond and the wooden barrier by the stream. Next turn left over the long wooden causeway. Arriving on the other side, do not take the path running half left up towards the houses, but go left along the edge of the pond. Pass some steps and a path going off to the right. Just before completing the circuit, turn right along the

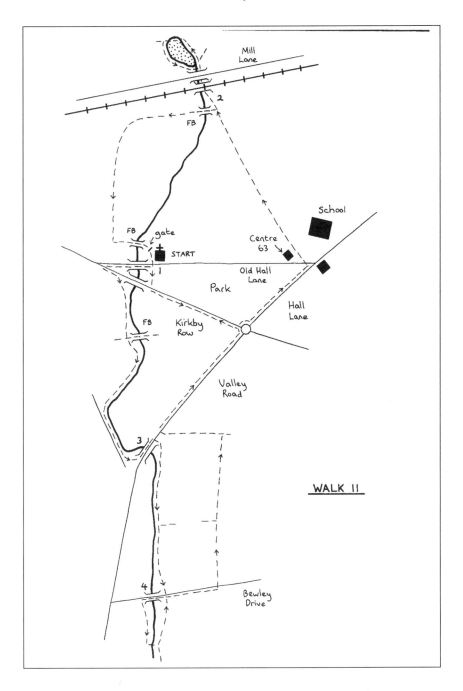

WALK II

right bank of the brook. As the path swings right by the hedge, carry on ahead, still by the brook, to reach Mill Lane again.

Turn left over the bridge, then right back, under the rail bridge. Instead of continuing along the tarmac path, keep by the edge of the brook to arrive at a footbridge. Over it, turn sharp right. Take the grass path to the left of the small stream. Do not follow the one to the right soon after, but bear left along the edge of the park. The path soon opens out, with houses to the right. Bear left across the grass to a footbridge over the stream, with a footpath sign guarding it. Over the bridge, turn immediately right off the tarmac path, along a narrow grass path. After passing a path going off to the right, you come to a gate in the churchyard wall. Through it, follow the path to the right of the church wall. At the war memorial, go ahead through the lych gate. This completes the first part of the loop.

Now turn right along Old Hall Lane. Cross Kirkby Row. Turn left to the bridge, then right along the grass on the right edge of the brook. This brings you to a footbridge, with two seats over to the right. Do not cross the bridge, but follow the tarmac path, which continues along the bank of the brook. Do not take either of two paths going up to the right, but continue until reaching Barn Lane. Turn left down the road to take the first path to the left.

3. Cross the dual carriageway, Valley Road. Turn left, crossing the bridge, then right along the tarmac path, now on the left edge of the stream, by the weeping willows. Pass a path going to the left. Carry on to reach Bewley Drive. Cross it to follow the footpath sign down the lane, with Ashton Downs estate on the left. Just before reaching Little Brook Cottage, turn right over the concrete bridge.

Turn sharp right to walk over the grassland to the left of the stream.

4. Back at Bewley Drive, turn right along the pavement. Go left, just before Bracknell Avenue on the right. Take the track with the fence on the right. Ignore the path to the left. Reaching a T-junction, turn left to follow the path as it runs along the side of a factory. Follow the path as it goes left downhill back to Valley Road. After crossing the road, stay on the grass verge, until arriving at the roundabout. Cross over the end of Kirkby Row to the left of the roundabout. Go through the entrance into St Chad's Park. Turn left along the perimeter path to arrive back at St Chad's Church.

12. Knowsley

The hidden oasis of Knowsley, with its village green, is at the centre of this easy walk.

Route: Pinfold Lane – Homer Wood – Gellings Farm – Croxteth Brook – Fluker's Brook Farm.

Starting Point: Alder Lane Knowsley. Grid reference: 433 951.

Distance: 3 miles.

Duration: 2 hours.

Map: Explorer 275.

By Car: Take the B5194 from junction 4 on the M57. On reaching Knowsley village centre green, turn right along Knowsley Lane. After passing the Derby Arms, the sign to look for is to the Kennels and Knowsley village shops. Where these point to the left, turn right into Pinfold Lane and immediately left into Alder Lane. The small car park, by Pear Tree Cottage, backs onto Knowsley Lane.

Refreshments: The Derby Arms on Knowsley Lane or The Knowsley in the centre (entrance in Mill Lane).

1. Walk back to Pinfold Lane, but this time turn left along it. Pass Maiden's Bower Farm on the left. The country lane makes its way by old cottages. As it bends to the left, Pinfold Wood, part of the Mersey Forest, is on the corner. A sign points to Knowsley post office. Continue along the lane, past a cottage on the right. The lane becomes more potholed beyond this point. Looking ahead towards Shepherd's Cottage, it is possible to see a footpath sign at the end of the lane. As you near the cottage, the sign disappears from view for a while. It is helpful to the less than confident to know that it is actually there.

Keep straight on past the front entrance to the cottage on your left. Straightway pass by the gate in front of you. The sign now directs you, away from the motorway ahead, to the right. This is towards what might seem the less than romantic destination of the Knowsley Industrial Estate. Do not be disappointed, because the wide green path is through fields populated by grazing horses. There is a stream to the right and a wire fence to the left. On arriving at a T-junction, by a bridge over the stream, follow the sign to the left, this time indicating Homer Wood as well as the Knowsley Industrial Estate. After following the path between the brook and the fence, continue along the edge of the field. St Mary's, Knowsley parish church, which was built in 1843, can be seen over to the right.

The path continues round the edge of Homer Wood. (There is a maze of paths in the wood, which can be accessed by taking the first path to the right after the commencement of the wood.) The wood edge path bears to the right to arrive at a picnic table and wood bridge over a stream. Cross the bridge, turn quickly left and right. Keep on the path on the wood edge. (Do not follow the path into the wood itself). Coming to the green perimeter fence of the industrial estate, turn left on the path. This brings you through the open field, along the side of the fence.

2. Over the stile at Delph Farm, turn right along the concrete road. To the right are stables. Then turn left down the dip as the road goes underneath the motorway. On the other side of the underpass, ignore the sign pointing left to Fluker's Brook Farm. The lane ahead, with fences on both sides, goes through fields. Coming to the bridge by Stand Lodge cottage, turn left along the bank of Croxteth Brook. At first, the grass track is wide, with houses to the right. When the wide track goes off to the right, by a culvert, stay on what is now a narrower path on the brook side. Shrubs and trees are to the right. Eventually houses appear back in view on the right. There are a few trees by the stream.

3. At the cross road of paths, with a stile ahead, turn left over the concrete bridge. The sign post points to Knowsley Lane. This is a wide stone track, with a brook on the left and fence on the right. Going though the gap on the left of the locked gate, turn right onto the tarmac road coming from the forbiddingly named Thunderbolt Cottages. The brook changes from the right side of the road to the left. After the small copse on the left, the road reaches the motorway. Turn right, following the Knowsley Lane sign, as the road runs parallel to the motorway. This is Fluker's Brook Lane. After passing the

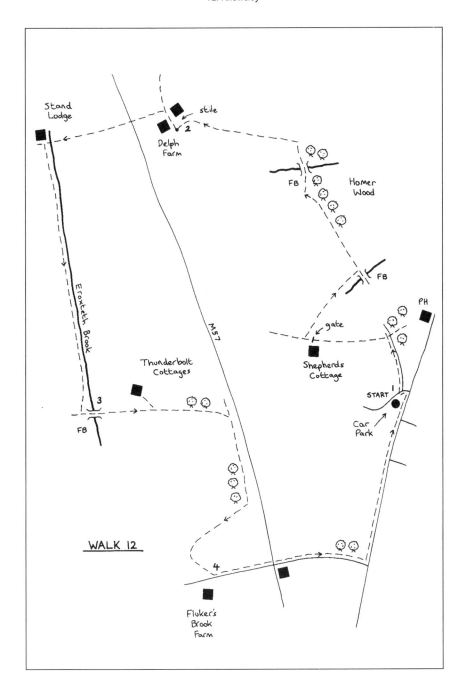

Stand
Lodge

stile

Delph
Farm

2

FB

Homer
Wood

FB

PH

gate

Shepherds
Cottage

START

Car
Park

Eroxteth Brook

M57

Thunderbolt
Cottages

3

FB

WALK 12

4

Fluker's
Brook
Farm

Knowsley Village Hall

wood known as The Roughs, the road swings up to the right away from the motorway.

4. By the sign stating 'Fluker's Brook Lane leading to Alder Lane – no through road', follow the sign post directing to Knowsley Lane, away from the farm, back over the motorway. This is Brook Lane, which passes a large house, Brookside, which is on your right. After the small wood, Akers Pit, the lane ends at a T-junction. Cross Knowsley Lane to the footpath on the far side. Go left, passing Home Farm Road. The car park is opposite to Sugar Lane.

13. Litherland

A walk through the tranquil valley of the River Rimrose, hidden amongst the urban surroundings of North Liverpool.

Route: Cooksons Bridge – Canal – Whabbs Common – Brook Vale Reserve – Cooksons Bridge.

Starting Point: Cooksons Bridge pub. Grid reference: 332 994.

Distance: 3 miles.

Duration: 1 hour or so.

Map: Explorer 275.

By Train: Seaforth and Litherland station is on the Merseyrail Northern line. From the station, turn right to the roundabout. Take the left exit. At the T-junction turn right and then left into Beach Road. At the end of Beach Road, pass through the gate to pick up the walk at point 2A.

By Car: Cooksons Bridge is by the canal bridge in Gorsey Lane (B5422) between Litherland and Netherton.

Refreshments: Cooksons Bridge public house.

---

1. From Cooksons Bridge, walk down the cobbled slope onto the canal towpath. It was the cutting of the canal in the late 18th century that brought prosperity to Litherland, with its a direct link with the port of Liverpool. Until then, it had grown little from the time it had been a 10th-century Norse hamlet. With housing on the far side of the water, there is woodland beyond the wooden fence. After passing a path to the right, at a second one, opposite to the canal turning basin, you come to open land.

Soon after a narrow quay, you pass under the new Brindley Bridge, which replaces the old walkway a few metres on. There is now a steel fence on the right and picnic tables. Large pylons can be seen ahead, as well as the cranes of Seaforth Docks in the distance. Then, after a single seat, follow the path that goes to the right from the towpath.

Cooksons Bridge Inn

2. This brings you onto Whabbs Common, as announced on the notice board. Take the path that bends to the left. This takes you to the right of the pylons, along the edge of woodland. At the crossroads of paths, turn left along the wide tarmac path.

At the next cross-path, turn left. Follow the path that bears right behind the pylon and in front of the picnic tables. This rejoins the tarmac path, where turn left towards the main gates.

Just before the gates, turn right in front of the notice board. Follow the path, going over the wooden bridge in the nature reserve. Continue forward, with trees and the stream on the right and a fence to the left. At the crossing of paths, go ahead, through the narrow gap in the fence into the Brook Vale wetland. At the path T-junction, turn right. The path passes the rail bridge to the left, joining the road. Go ahead, passing the two playing field pavilions, which are to the right.

3. At the entrance to the Brook Vale playing fields, turn right. Go across in front of the pavilion, to the wooden fence. Follow the fence, passing two paths coming up from the lower playing field. At the corner of the playing field, a path leads back onto the parkland. Do not follow the worn path to the right, but aim left onto a gravel track. This takes you along the top edge of the playing field bound-

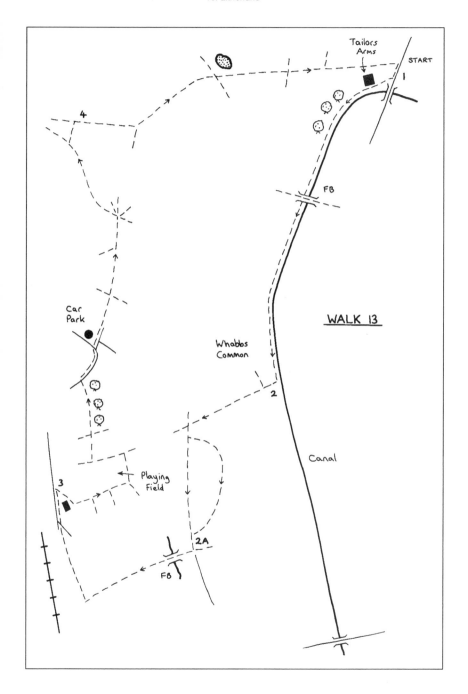

ary shrubs. At the intersection of paths, turn left. This path goes down the other boundary of the playing field. At the open entrance into the playing field, leave the gravel path to go right along a grass track, which reaches another gravel path at the corner of a plantation. Cross the path, to follow the line of trees, with the plantation to the right and goal posts to the left. Come onto the wide track, bearing to the right. As it bears to the left, go straight across by the end of the car park (at the end of the tarmac path) onto a gravel path going uphill.

After going ahead at the crossroads, and ignoring a left turn, turn first left at the five ways. There are plantations on both sides. Do not take the path that bears left, but go straight on as the path, with a short stretch of wooden fencing to either side, meets at a T-junction.

4. Turn right up the path and then left on a wide dirt track. Pass a crossroads and a pond on the left. Then straight on at the crossroads, by the Valley wetlands sign. The Tailors Arms pub is now in sight ahead. Continue straight on, passing a path coming in from the wetlands on the left. The path now runs along the side of a fence to the left. On emerging onto the road, turn right for the hundred metres back to the starting point.

14. Liverpool: 1

The Victorian heritage of Liverpool is noticeable on this city walk.

Route: Pier Head – Victoria Monument – St George's Hall – Town Hall – St Nicholas Church – Pier Head.

Starting Point: Port of Liverpool Building, Pier Head. Grid reference: 339 901.

Distance: 3 miles.

Duration: 2 hours.

Map: Explorer 275.

By Train: James Street Merseyrail station. Pick up the walk at instruction number 2.

By Car: There is a car park left off Mann Island, almost opposite the Port of Liverpool Building.

Refreshments: Numerous restaurants and pubs en route.

---

1. From the Pier Head, walk to the right of the Port of Liverpool Building. Cross the Strand, to walk up James Street.

The red brick and stone house on the corner is Albion House. This was built in 1898 by R.N. Shaw and J.F. Doyle for Thomas Ismay's White Star shipping company. Shaw also designed New Scotland Yard in London. The striped pattern is reminiscent of that of a liner.

2. Passing the Merseyrail station on the left, arrive in Derby Square. In front of the Queen Elizabeth law courts stands the imposing monument commemorating Queen Victoria.

This was built five years after her death in 1906. The four representations are Industry, Agriculture, Commerce and Education. Before this, the site was occupied by St George's church until its demolition in 1897. In turn, the church had replaced Liverpool Castle, which stood here from 1235 to 1721. A replica, built by Lord Leverhulme, can be seen at Rivington, near Bolton.

From Derby Square, head along the pedestrianised Lord Street. Turn left into North John Street, then second right into Mathew Street. Does any know why it is only spelled with one 't'? We are now entering Beatle Land.

The Victoria Monument

On the left is the Cavern Pub. The figure of John Lennon is beside his 'Liddypool' ditty. Chiselled into the exterior brickwork are the names of the many groups, known and unknown, who performed in and around Liverpool in the early 60s. Almost immediately after, on the right, is the Cavern Club, a replica of the original Cavern. Almost on the same site, it is built from the original bricks. Moving on, high up on the wall on the left, is the Beatle Street sculpture of the late Arthur Dooley, a local artist. Next, to the right, is Cavern Walks. Inside, in the refreshment area, is a statue to 'the four lads who shook the world'. The doves and the rose emblems on the outside were designed by Cynthia Lennon. Continuing down the street, on the left is a favourite haunt of the Beatles, the Grapes pub.

At the end of Mathew Street, turn left into Stanley Street.

You have not quite left the Beatles behind. On the right is the figure of Eleanor Rigby, dedicated to 'all the lonely people'. On reaching Victoria Street, turn left. On the corner of Temple Court, opposite to Temple Lane is Fowlers building, built by James Picton in 1864. Now go back along Victoria, past Stanley Street again. After passing the rear of the Conservation Centre, turn right along Crosshall. Ahead is

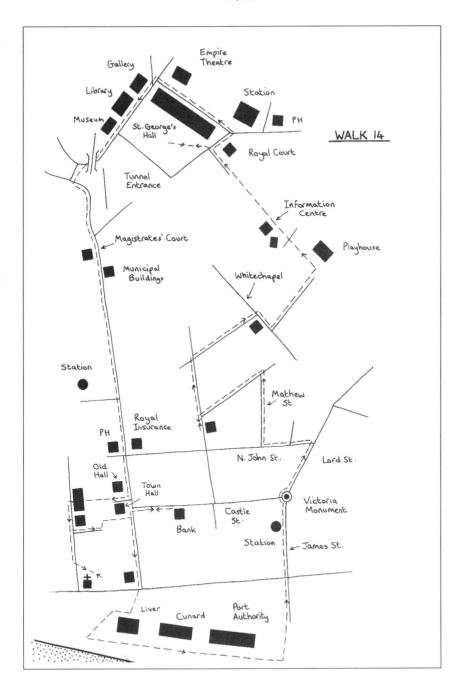

WALK 14

the new development of Queen Square. Turn right again in front of the Conservation Centre. Housed in a Victorian warehouse, the Centre is open Monday to Saturday 10.00am – 5.00pm and Sunday 12 noon – 5.00pm. It is closed 23-6 December and 1 January. Besides housing two celebrated local statues, Eros and the Spirit of Liverpool, two Beatles gold discs and a rare copy of the Mona Lisa, conservators can be seen at work restoring anything from paintings to space suits.

Go across the pedestrian crossing, with Yates Wine Lodge on the far side. Then go left up Dawson Street. Cross Williamson Square, which was surrounded by houses when it was built in the 18th century. Ahead is the newly refurbished Playhouse, with the Radio City Tower rising behind it.

The Playhouse was formerly known as The Star. Opening in 1865, it claims to be the first repertory theatre in Britain. Turn left in front of the theatre. Under the bridge and past the Information Office, come into Roe Street. The Royal Court Theatre is to the right. Cross the road and up the steps to the left of St George's Hall. This is St John's Gardens, named after the church and graveyard on the site until 1897. It was originally proposed that the Anglican Cathedral should be built here. Statues to Liverpool worthies litter the Gardens. Immediately at the back of the hall stand memorials to A. B. Forwood and William Rathbone. Near to the memorial to soldiers who have died during the troubles in Northern Ireland is the statue of Rodney Street born W.E. Gladstone, four times Prime Minister. In the bottom part of the Gardens are statues remembering Church of England, Rev. Major Lester, Vicar of Kirkdale, and Roman Catholic Father James Nugent, both 19th-century philanthropists. They flank a memorial to the Kings Regiment, closely connected with Liverpool.

Now walk round the right end of the Hall to the opposite side in Lime Street.

On the other side of the road are four notable buildings. Going from left to right, first is the Empire Theatre, built in 1925 in a style sympathetic to the Hall opposite, replaced a previous theatre. Next to it is the old North Western Hotel designed in French Renaissance style in 1871. It is now used by John Moores University. Behind it is

St George's Hall

Lime Street station. This was opened in 1836, being connected to Edge Hill station by a tunnel cut through the rock. The present station dates from 1869, when it boasted the largest roof span in the world. It was refurbished in 2000. On the corner of Lime Street and Skelhorne Street, the Crown Hotel of 1905 is of art nouveau design. The plaster work carries both the name of the pub and that of Walkers Ales. Some of the money that Mr Walker made from his brewing was spent on the Art Gallery that bears his name.

Now cross back to the Hall.

490 feet long, it was designed by Harvey Lonsdale Elmes, who, at the age of 25, won competitions for both the hall and an assize court. Both were combined into one building, which was completed in 1854. Inside, the great hall has a barrel roof. The floor of Minton tiles is only uncovered for public viewing for a few days each year. The concert hall, with its Willis organ, was designed by C.R. Cockerall. He completed the whole project after Elmes' early death.

In front of the steps, the war memorial separates the statues of Queen Victoria and Prince Albert. On the steps themselves are the statues of William Earle, in military uniform and Benjamin Disraeli, twice Conservative Prime Minister.

From the front of the hall, walk towards the statue of the Duke of Wellington.

This was made from gun metal from Wellington's victory at Waterloo in 1805. Adjacent to it is the cast-iron Steble Fountain, donated in 1879 by a former mayor of that name. Immediately in front of you is Islington. Opposite the Wellington statue is the Sessions House built in classical style by F. and G. Holme in 1882 – 4. To its left is the Walker Art Gallery of 1877 named after its benefactor Andrew Walker, the brewer. There are a number of Italian Renaissance paintings, which were part of William Roscoe's collection and the works of George Stubbs, the Liverpool equine artist. It opened in 1877, with extensions in 1882 and 1931. The statues in front of the building are of Raphael and Michelangelo. Next to it the stands the William Brown Library and Museum of 1860 in the street named after the rich local merchant. The Picton Reading Room, with its dome, is an integral part of the building. Based on the old British Museum reading room, it was named after James Picton, the chairman of the country's first library committee. Opened in 1879, Cornelius Sherlock was the architect. Lastly is the College of Technology and Museum extension of 1902.

Immediately ahead is the entrance to Queensway, the older of the two Mersey road tunnels. It took from 1925 to 1934 to complete, has a 44 ft diameter tube, and is 2.13 miles long. The entrance decoration is 1930s art deco style by A. L. Rowse.

Take the crossing to the right of the roundabout, over the dual carriageway and under the flyover to the start of Dale Street.

Note on the right, next to Trueman Street, no 139 in a short row of 18th-century town houses. It is said to be the best example of a period town house left in the city. Just after the end of the flyover on the right is the Magistrates' Court, built in 1859. Almost opposite, on the corner of Crosshall Street, is the renaissance style Municipal Building and Annexe, completed in 1866. Both were designed by John Weightman, the city surveyor.

On the near corner of Temple Street is the red-brick Prudential Assurance. Looking up the street opposite, you will see in the distance the retained facade of the old Exchange Station. The golden dome of the Royal Insurance building of 1903 is on the near corner of North John Street. It was designed by J Francis Doyle, being based on a frame of steel and an exterior of granite and Portland stone. High on the North John Street side of the building is a sundial dated 1903. Opposite to North John Street are two of Liverpool's oldest streets, Leather Lane and Hackins Hey. The latter contains, on its right-hand side, Ye Hole in Ye Wall pub of 1726. At nos. 8-10 is the Queen Insurance building of 1839. The first floor pillars give an air of solidarity. The royal coat of arms indicates its previous use as the Royal Bank.

Soon after this, you will reach the splendid Town Hall.

This was opened in 1754, having been designed by John Wood the Elder. After a fire in 1795, James Wyatt carried out refurbishment, at which time he added a dome surmounted by the figure of Minerva. The chandeliers of the ballroom weigh more than one tonne each.

On the corner of Dale Street and High Street is the 1877 Liverpool, London and Globe Insurance Building, on which a plaque states that this was the site of the first Town Hall.

Walk across the road to the corner of Dale Street and Castle Street.

Here is the Midland Bank building built in 1863. Cross Castle Street, walking as far as the present Nat. West Bank. Set in the wall is a plaque referring to the Sanctuary Stone. It states that it is one of two sanctuary stones, which defined the precincts of the old Liverpool fair. The building itself is of striking bands of red sandstone and granite. It was opened as the Albany Bank in 1892.

Walk back to the Town Hall, along High Street to its right, into Exchange Flags.

The name comes from the fact that the Town Hall was originally intended as an exchange. In the centre is Nelson's monument, sculpted by Richard Westmacott. Dating from 1813, it is the city's oldest. 'England expects every man to do his duty' is emblazoned on it. The base of the statue also served as a ventilation shaft for the bonded warehouse that was below. The four figures came from the Dublin Parliament. Go ahead through the main doors onto Tithebarn Street. Turn left, continuing ahead into Chapel Street. Pass the 19th-century Pig and Whistle pub and Hargreaves Building, on the

corner of Covent Garden, on the left. The latter was built by James
Picton in 1859. The busts on the outside are of Christopher Columbus
and other South American explorers.

Just before St Nicholas' church, turn left into the graveyard.

The church of Our Lady and St Nicholas has been on this site since at
least the 13th century. St Nicholas is the patron saint of sailors, so it
is known as the Sailors Church. The rocket-shaped tower was built in
1815. This replaced one that killed 23 worshippers when it fell down.
The nave was rebuilt in 1952 after war damage. On the far side of the
graveyard is the Tower Building. It is so called because the Tower of
Liverpool was on the site until 1819. Built in 1908 by W. Aubrey
Thomas, it was a steel frame construction with glazed tiles, which
withstood the grime of the polluted atmosphere. Retrace your steps
to the corner of Rumford Street, noting on the left a plaque on the
left-hand side recalling the site of Richmond Buildings, which James
Picton had built for William Brown. Walk along Rumford Street,
passing Derby House. During World War 2, the basement was the
control centre for the Western approaches. It directed the protection
of merchant ships against enemy attack during the Battle of the
Atlantic. The operations room, admiral's office and teleprinter station
are open to the public.

Turn left into Exchange Passage West, which brings you into
Exchange Flags again. Turn first right into Exchange Street West to
come out in Water Street. Immediately on the right is the old Mar-
tins Bank (now Barclays).

The Portland Stone building in French classical style, dates from
1932. The architect, Herbert Rowse, knew the USA well, so the glass
ceiling and low banking hall give have a transatlantic flavour. Pass the
bank and Rumford Street. On the corner of the next street, Covent
Garden, is no 14, Oriel Buildings. This caused much debate when built
in 1864 by Peter Ellis, as the plaque at the entrance informs us. Its
design was much ahead of its time, given the steel frame, tall oriel
windows and narrow decorated mullions. This is one of the city's most
important buildings in that it was the precursor of modern design.
The huge 1923 India Buildings opposite were also by Rowse. He built it

in 1931 for the Holt Blue Funnel Line, which had been founded in 1865. It is on the site of the India Buildings of 1833, whose name commemorated the ending of the monopoly of the East India Company. The inside is palatial with a barrel vaulted arcade and marble inlaid floor.

From the bottom of Water Street, walk across the Strand.

The river front was here, until the first docks were built. Also in this area was the Goree warehouses, connected with the slave trade. Turn right along George's Dock Gates. At the end of the buildings, go left, past the stone pillar, marked Mersey Dock Gate 1873 and to the right of the brick buildings. Ahead, by Prince's Landing Stage, is what is known as the Titanic memorial, but in fact commemorates all marine engine crews who perished at sea. Go left across the little bridge onto the large area of the Pier Head, which was built on the site of George's dock. The bandstand commemorates those killed on convoy work during the World War 2. The left of the three buildings is the Royal Liver Building. This was built between 1908-11. Designed by W. Aubrey Thomas, it was one of the first high structures constructed with reinforced concrete. Above its eight storeys, are the largest clock faces in the country. Perched on top of the building are the Liver Birds, from which the city takes its name. Their German designer was rewarded by being imprisoned on the Isle of Man at the outbreak of the Second World War.

In the centre is the 1916 Cunard Building of rusticated Portland stone. Designed by Willink and Thicknesse in Italian Renaissance style, it has a memorial to staff who died in the First World War at the entrance. Until 1966, it watched the great liners of the company arriving and departing from the port.

The third building is the Port of Liverpool building of 1907. This is the headquarters of the Mersey Docks and Harbour Board. In front of the buildings is a statue of Edward VII on horseback. By the restaurant and bar in front of the entrance to the Mersey Ferries is another statue. This commemorates Alfred Lewis Jones, the founder of the Liverpool School of Tropical Medicine.

You are now back at the starting point.

15. Liverpool: 2

A walk to the south of the city centre. Two 20th-century cathedrals vie with the magnificence of the 19th-century Albert Dock for pre-eminence.

Route: Albert Dock – Anglican Cathedral – Catholic Cathedral – Adelphi – Albert Dock.

Starting Point: Information Centre, Albert Dock. Grid Reference: 343 898.

Distance: 2 miles.

Duration: 1 hour.

Map: Explorer 275.

By Train: From James Street Merseyrail station, walk down James Street. At the bottom, turn left along The Strand to reach the Albert Dock.

By Car: Drive south from the Pier Head along The Stand and Wapping. After passing the Albert Dock, turn right to find a large parking area.

Refreshments: Available at the Albert Dock.

---

1. You will possibly wish to leave your wandering around the Albert Dock area until the end of the walk. Starting from the information centre walk left between the buildings and the Salthouse Dock. At the end of the dock, turn right, with Canning Dock on the left, to the road. Cross directly over into Canning Place.

This was the site of Liverpool's first dock, completed by William Steers in 1815. By looking along Park Lane, which is first on the right, you can see the Swedish Seaman's Church, erected early in the 20th century. This is evidence of the cosmopolitan nature of this international seaport at that time. It is reputed to have a replica in Hamburg.

Walk to the junction of Paradise Street, Hanover Street and Duke Street. On the corner of the first two named is Church House.

This is the headquarters of the Liverpool Anglican Diocese. Before

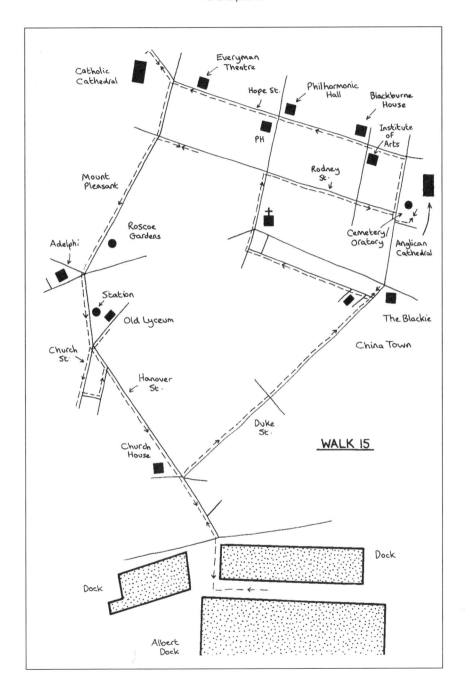

WALK 15

that the church base was in North John Street until the building was bombed during World War

2. Turn right up Duke Street. At the top of Duke Street, look to the right.

The recently built archway is the entrance to the Chinatown area. This is the oldest Chinese community in the Europe dating back to the mid-19th century. On the corner is the old church building, affectionately known as the Blackie. This was because of the grimy appearance it used to have before it was cleaned up. Once the cathedral of the Congregation church, it is now an arts centre.

Go back down Duke Street to turn first right into Colquitt Street.

On the left, between Parr Street and Seel Street is the Royal Institution, built in 1799. It was started by William Roscoe, a great local patron of the arts. On reaching Bold Street, turn right.

Facing you at the top of Bold Street are the substantial ruins of St Luke's church. Completed in 1831, it suffered damage during World War

Chinatown

2. The roofless building has not been used for worship since then. It acts as an unofficial memorial to the many who died and were injured during bombing raids.

The way ahead now lies up Leece Street, to the left of the church. At the traffic lights turn right into Rodney Street, so called after Rodney, the naval admiral.

The street, the other half of which is to the left, is notable for its medical practitioners. It is known as the Harley Street of Liverpool. The architecture is a fascinating mixture of styles of door-cases, porticoes and balconies. Walking along the street, you will pass no 34, where lived Henry Booth (1789 – 1869) founder of the Liverpool – Manchester railway. No 35 is thought to have been the first house to be built in Rodney Street. William Roscoe lived here from 1783 – 4. At no 43 resided Thurston Holland (1863 – 1941), who was a pioneer in radiology. No 54 was the home Dr Duncan, Liverpool's first Medical Officer of Health from 1847 – 63. His was the first such post in the country. No 62 was the birthplace of William Ewart Gladstone, the Liberal Prime Minister, in 1808. The house had been built 12 years earlier, at the time being a detached residence.

At the end of Rodney Street, cross over Upper Duke Street to the massive Anglican Cathedral.

This is probably the last great Gothic-style cathedral to be built in Britain. There had not been a cathedral on a new site since the 13th century. Commenced in 1904, the Lady Chapel was completed in 1910. The young architect Giles Gilbert Scott constantly revised his plans. At one stage, the cathedral was to have had twin towers. Scott was also the designer of one of the smallest creations, the red telephone box. One such is at the top of the Western Room steps to point up the contrast with his cathedral. Scott did not live to see the completion of his masterpiece in 1978. The nave bridge was an innovation, which complemented the soaring spaciousness of the pillar-less interior. The largest cathedral in Europe, the peal of bells lays claim to the heaviest in the world. A trip up the 331ft tower enables widespread views over the city and well beyond.

Opposite to the main entrance to the Cathedral is the Oratory built in 1829, which acted as the mortuary for the cemetery. It is open to the public from 2.30-4.00pm on Saturday afternoons between 1 April and 31 October. Described as 'a miniature acropolis', it was designed in the style of a Greek temple by John Foster. It would be a pity to leave the cathedral area without a look at St James' cemetery. The same John Foster had the idea that Pevsner, the architectural historian, has called "a stroke of genius". Here on St James Mount had been a quarry, which had provided stone for the building of the Town Hall. On its closure in 1825, Foster decided to turn it into a cemetery for St James's church, lower down Upper Parliament Street on the other side of the Cathedral. Entrance to it is by a steep gravestone-lined path from in front of the Oratory. Before descending, view the earlier 19th-century houses of Gambier Terrace, above the opposite side of the cemetery. From the grounds of the cemetery, the view of the Cathedral, high above, is overpowering. By the time the cemetery closed in 1936, there were over 50,000 bodies buried there. One of the most famous was William Huskinson, the MP for the city who was knocked down and killed by Stephenson's Rocket on its first journey in 1830 at the opening of the Liverpool to Manchester line. He is commemorated by a 1836 rotunda containing a statue. Amongst others buried here are William Brown and Kitty Wilkinson. One of the sea captains commemorated is Captain Halsey of Carolina who died in 1844. His grave is complete with its star-spangled banner. A grave of the Keay family, complete with the places where its members died, records the important trade links between Liverpool, USA and Africa.

From the cathedral, turn right up Upper Duke Street. Turn left into Hope Street.

At the junction with Mount Street is an original piece of sculpture. In 1998, LIPA commissioned John King to do the sculpture of piles of cases, which is on the pavement. Funding was provided by the National Lottery. The notice of the railings is a guide to the 'Case History', indicating the well-known Liverpudlian to which the initials on each case refers. A few metres down Mount Street is the imposing facade of what used to be the Liverpool Institute, built in 1825. The school building is now the home of the Liverpool Institute for

Performing Arts, founded by Beatle Paul McCartney, a former pupil at the school.

Standing back from the road, on the opposite side of Hope Street from the pile of cases, is Blackburne House. This is named after a mayor of Liverpool, John Blackburne, who had it built towards the end of the 18th century. Until the late 20th century, it was in use as a girls' grammar school. At the corner of Hope Street and Myrtle Street is the Philharmonic Hall, home of the Royal Liverpool Philharmonic Orchestra. Built in 1939 to a design of Henry Rowse, a major interior renovation took place in 1999. On the opposite corner is the Philharmonic pub. Dating from 1900, it not only serves as a refuge for exhausted musicians, but is also a work of elaborate art. The ornate gate was a joint effort by pupils of the Liverpool School of Arts. The interior, lavishly designed by Walter Thomas, is a rich ornate mixture of ornamental work of wood, metal, stone and marble. The gents' toilets are extravagantly designed. A pity the ladies are not allowed to see them.

Further down Hope Street, on the right, you will pass the Everyman Theatre. Originally a 19th-century church, it became a theatre in 1964.

At the end of Hope Street, cross over the road to the Roman Catholic Cathedral.

Of Sir Edward Lutyens' pre-war grand design for a cathedral larger than St Paul's, only the crypt was completed. The architect, Sir Frederick Gibberd, an Anglican, designed a simpler, modern building. It took only five years to build, being consecrated in 1967. Known affectionately as Paddy's Wigwam, it is circular in shape, with a central marble altar. Around the edge of the circle are numerous chapels. A suffused light of brilliant colours comes from the glass lantern. Weighing in at 1000 tonnes, it was the design of John Piper.

From the Cathedral, with the buildings of the University to the left, return along Mount Pleasant. At the junction with Hope Street, turn right. This is still Mount Pleasant. At the junction with Rodney Street, turn left.

This half of the street is not as architecturally interesting as the first half we looked at. On the left, note first the rather forlorn St Andrew's church, built in 1823. The pyramid on the right of the building is the burial place of a gambler called Mackenzie, who apparently requested that he be interred in a standing position. No. 9, was the home in the 19th century of the poet, Arthur Clough and his sister Anne, the first principal of Newnham College, Cambridge.

4. Back to Mount Pleasant, turn left. Just after passing the YMCA, note the Roscoe Memorial Gardens.

These commemorate one of Liverpool's illustrious alumni, William Roscoe (1753-1831). The area was a former burial ground, Roscoe being one of many buried here. At the bottom of the road, where it meets Lime Street and Renshaw Street, the Adelphi Hotel is a reminder of Liverpool's days of liner glory. Many a passenger on one of the great transatlantic ships would have stayed here. Built in 1912, the architect was Frank Atkinson, who also designed Selfridges in London. Opposite, on the corner of Ranelagh Street, is Lewis's store, presided over by the sculpture of a nude man, by Jacob Epstein. Continue down Ranelagh Street, passing the entrance to Central Station. Before turning right into Church Street, notice on the left-hand corner of Bold Street, the Lyceum. Now a post office, it was built in 1802 to contain Liverpool Library. This had been started in 1758 as part of a gentlemen's club and coffee house. At the time, it was the first subscription library in Europe.

(If time is running out at this stage, a short cut is to walk on down Hanover Street.) Otherwise, proceed along Church Street, past the statues of John and Peter Moores. Soon after the left turning to the Bluecoat Chambers, look for a star in the pavement outside the HMV shop.

This was the site of St Peter's church, the 'church' of Church Street, which was the Anglican pro-Cathedral until the building of the Cathedral. Retrace your steps to Church Alley to approach the Bluecoat Chambers. Built in 1717, it was the Bluecoat School for a number of years. These days it is a centre for the arts. To its right is the Athenaeum Club. From the Bluecoat, turn left to arrive in Hanover Street. Go right to reach Church House, on the corner of Paradise

Street. From here, continue down Hanover Street, back to the Albert Dock.

The Albert Dock was the creation of Jesse Hartley, who was the Dock Engineer from 1824 – 60. The advanced technology of the time included the use of brick and iron, helping to make it fireproof. The installation of hydraulic machinery meant much more efficient loading of cargo. The dock was opened by Prince Albert himself in 1845. After being empty for years, the area was renovated. It now includes shops, the Beatles Story, the Merseyside Maritime Museum and the Tate Gallery of modern art.

16. Mersey and The Three Parks

A classic walk along the banks of the Mersey and the pride of Liverpool, its rolling acres of parkland.

Route: Albert Dock – Riverside Walk – Otterspool Promenade – Otterspool Park – Sefton Park – Princes Park – Princes Road – Albert Dock.

Starting Point: The car park at the end of Mann Island, adjacent to the Pier Head. Grid reference: 339 901.

Distance: 6 miles.

Duration: 3 hours.

Map: Explorer 275.

By Train: The nearest Merseyrail station is James Street. From the station turn right down James Street. Cross over the dual carriageway, directly into Mann Island.

By Car: Mann Island is immediately south of the Port of Liverpool Building, opposite James Street.

Refreshments: Brittania pub and The Otterspool pub on Otterspool Promenade and the café in Sefton Park.

---

1. From the Mann Island car park, walk towards the Maritime Museum. To the left is Canning Dock, with its display of ships. Turn right in front of the Museum, then left across the bridge of the Half Tide Dock. The riverside walkway then runs between the waterfront and the vast buildings surrounding Albert Dock. Pass the flagpole at the end of the buildings. Go straight on over the inlet, along Kings Parade, which runs along the waterfront.

The large Albert Dock car park is to the left. In the distance, away to the left, can be seen the two cathedrals as well as the tower of St Luke's church. On the other side of the river, Cammell Laird's ship builders loom large.

The large bulk of the modern Customs and Excise building is next on the left. At the road junction turn right along Mariners Wharf. You are

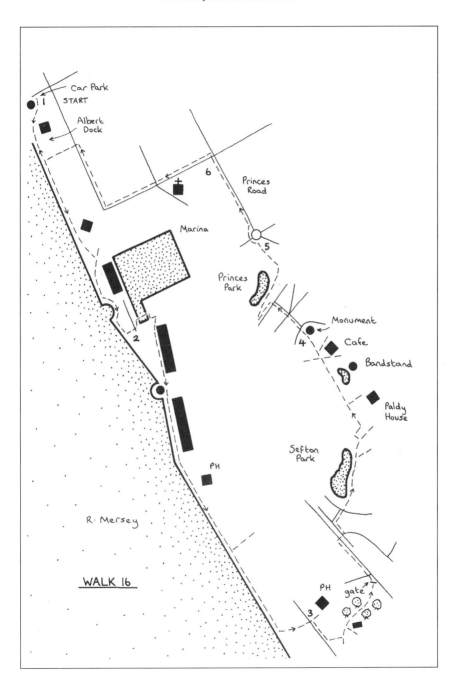

WALK 16

R. Mersey

Car Park
START
Albert Dock
Marina
Princes Road
Princes Park
Monument
Cafe
Bandstand
Paldy House
Sefton Park
gate
PH

now entering the new apartments and houses of the Riverside Village. Behind the apartments on the left is the Marina. Follow the next inlet round onto Quebec Quay to continue along the river side walk. Passing over the next inlet, you will notice a boat yard on the left, behind a large monumental anchor.

2. Coming to a turning circle after the next set of apartments, cross directly over to the pedestrian swing bridge over Brunswick Lock. Follow the walkway to the right, then quickly left and right again. Pass through a gate, bearing a notice advising that it is open 8.00am until 7.00pm or sunset. The next length of the riverside has high railings on the left, dividing it from the Brunswick Industrial Estate. Along the way are numerous seats.

As the buildings end, look over to the left. The end building has the erection date of 1887 written on it. Beyond the clock tower can be seen the towering edifice of Wilson's Flour Mill on Mill Street, Toxteth.

With now more buildings to the left, pass a round stone marking the site of the southern basin of the old Harrington Dock, dated 1885. Ahead, on the small promontory, is a building converted into the Chung Fu restaurant. Go to the left of it, aiming for the monumental anchor ahead.

Over in the distance to the left, up in the rock face is the mouth of a tunnel. This is one of the few remaining signs of the old Overhead Railway, which ran along the dock front to Seaforth in the north. Its southern terminus was at Dingle at the other end of the tunnel.

The riverside walk continues from the anchor, with new offices and apartments on the left. Next, pass a flagpole, besides two ships' ventilators. Stay on the walkway by the river, passing another anchor, then a blue star funnel.

You are now on the Dingle Esplanade as the 1983 sign on a plaque indicates. All of this area along the front was upgraded as the site of the 1984 Liverpool Garden Festival. The maritime theme is continued with another funnel. The Britannia pub is now arrived at.

On the walkway in front of the pub, are placed stars, indicating the names of many Merseyside entertainers and sports people, including the Grand National legend, Red Rum. Just beyond the pub, a map by

The bandstand, Sefton Park

the walkway indicates places of interest on the other side of the river. This is the point at which Otterspool Promenade joins the Marine Esplanade.

After the large buoy, a signpost indicates the direction of St Michael's station to the left for anyone who wants to shorten the walk. The buildings of the water board, surrounded by incongruous glaring red railings, leads on to a lonely mizzen mast. There are now a number of tarmac paths off to the left. Look out for the one that has a platform of seats near it. Take the branch to the right of the seats. The path gives out at the top of the slope. Walk straight ahead across the grass to the Otterspool pub.

3. Unless you are going to take a break at this point, turn right in front of the surrounds of the pub. Follow the tarmac path, until you see the Otterspool Park sign on your left. Do not take the dirt track going away at 90% to the left. Instead, take the tarmac path going downwards at an angle to the left. At the crossroads turn left to go towards the building in the distance, passing *en route* a path going to the right. Pass the sadly neglected 1930s style old cafeteria. Many a Liverpudlian has happy memories of coming here for ice-cream and lollypops in its heyday. Let's hope these days will return.

On the other side of the building is a very wide path, with railings on the right-hand side. Stay on this, as you pass under a bridge, to go on through the tree laden little valley. At one point, there is a rock face on the left. The path gradually veers to the left, then straightens up to bring you to some gates. Through these, go up the short stretch of road to arrive at traffic lights at the junction of Jericho Lane and Aigburth Road. Cross the road to find, a few metres ahead, an underpass. This takes you under the Aigburth Road dual carriageway. On the other side, turn left. Cross the road, with Aigburth Vale to the right of you. Continue left, walking by the side of the railings, towards the entrance to Sefton Park. Do not take the short slip road that bears left back to Aigburth Road.

The 269 acres of Sefton Park were landscaped between 1867 and 1872 by architects Edouard Andre and Louis Hornblower.

In the park, make for the ornate water fountain in front of the boating lake. This is directly ahead on the other side of the perimeter road (Aigburth Drive). Follow the path that goes along the right edge of the lake. Stay on it until you reach the other end. Do not take the path that goes uphill to the right, but stay by the fence until you reach steps ahead. Turn left in front of them, over the stepping stone to go up the steps immediately ahead. On the plateau at the top of the steps is a statue. Turn right to reach a wide tarmac path. Go left, with railings on the left and water below.

Over to the right can be seen the newly refurbished Palm House. Originally erected in 1896, it suffered much vandalism in recent years. The renovations have cost in the region of £200,000. The building can be reached by taking the first path to the right.

Otherwise, keep straight ahead on the main path, ignoring the two to the right and the one coming in from the left. After this, the railings and the water are on your right. On a small island in the water can be seen a bandstand. On reaching the large piazza, dominated by an emblazoned fountain, a rest may be taken at the café. A number of paths radiate out from here. Aim for the one ahead, second left of the café. There is a steel signpost on the left at its commencement, pointing on to Princes Park half a mile away. The path runs through an avenue of trees towards the tall monument in the distance. The bowling green on the left is passed.

4. At the monument, go ahead beyond the roundabout to the traffic lights. A Liverpool loop line sign points the way. Take the narrower side road opposite to the lights. At the T-junction, turn left into Windermere Terrace, passing St Gabriel's House and Bellerive Sixth Form College. As the road ends, carry on into Princes Park.

Princes Park was the first of Liverpool's parks in 1842. Its architect was James Paxton, the designer of the Crystal Palace. In fact, the park was a prototype for parks all over the world. Soon afterwards Paxton was responsible for laying out Birkenhead Park, which was the source of inspiration for Central Park in New York. Turn right immediately after entry to follow the path to the right round the edge of the lake. At the end of the lake carry on up to the T-junction in front of the houses. Turn left along the wide path to reach the park gates.

5. With a roundabout in front of you, go ahead along the wide boulevard. The road to the left of the central space is Princes Road; the one to the right of it Princes Avenue. The grand Victorian houses on either side are gradually being refurbished to bring them back to something like their former glories.

Immediately after the two parallel roads join into one, look out for some interesting buildings. On the right is the Jewish synagogue. Built in 1874, this replaced the previous meeting place in Seel Street. The large Rose window can be seen from the road. It has a vaulted nave roof. Next to it is St Margaret's Anglican church. This was built by the famous ecclesiastical architect G. E. Street. A local high churchman, Douglas Horsfall, provided the money, which he also did for St Agnes Church in Ullet Road. Towards the end of the 19th century, St Margaret's was involved in great controversy over its high church practices. So much so that its vicar, Bell-Cox, spent some time in Walton goal. On reaching the corner of Upper Hampton Street, look directly across to the Greek Orthodox Church.

6. At the traffic lights, turn left along Upper Parliament Street. Pass by the end of Windsor Street, with the vast bulk of the Anglican Cathedral over to the right. At the junction with St James' Place, notice on your left St James's Church.

The author was present at the last meeting of its church council before closure in 1969. Since then it has been in the care of the Council for Redundant Churches. It is still looking for a purpose in life, whilst being patched up to prevent it falling down. This is an unfortunate state for one of the most important ecclesiastical structures in the city. Although the chancel was not added until the end of the 19th century, the rest of the building dates from 1774. Based on a cast iron structure, it was one of the first to be erected in that material. Other examples in the city are St George's Everton and St Michael's in the Hamlet, Aigburth. The architect behind this revolution in building was Thomas Rickman (1776-1841). Quentin Hughes notes that the use of cast iron enabled a building to be erected quickly and to be fireproof.

At the crossroads, continue down Parliament Street, with the river ahead. Bear right at the bottom. On reaching the main entrance to the Albert Dock car park, walk across to the waterfront. Turn right to reach the Mann Island car park along the same stretch as the outward route.

17. Lydiate

The ruins of an old hall and its chapel, two churches and a rail track feature in this walk.

Route: Our Lady's Church – St Thomas' Church – Acres Lane – Cheshire Lines Path – Our Lady's Church.

Starting Point: Our Lady's R.C. Church Lydiate. Grid reference 365 053.

Distance: 4 miles.

Duration: 2 hours.

Map: Explorer 285.

By Train: None.

By Car: The church is on the corner of the A567 road and Hall Lane. There is room to park in Hall Lane or in the grounds of Old Hall Farm opposite, if using the farm shop or restaurant.

Refreshments: At Old Hall Farm.

---

1. Old Hall Farm has a lot to offer. There is a lovely old farm building, by the duck pond, now turned into a cafeteria. Another old building houses the farm shop. To the left of the farm shop are the ruins of Lydiate Hall. Sefton Council has cleared the area, so that it is possible to walk around the ruins. There is a useful information board. A visit before or after the walk is rewarding.

The oldest part of Lydiate Hall was the east wing. This was pulled down in the 18ᵗʰ century. It is thought that some of the stone was used to erect the building that houses the farm shop. The house was lived in by the Ireland family for a number of centuries. The church of Our Lady was built as a replacement for St Katherine's chapel in 1854. Alabaster panels in the interior, depicting the martyrdom of St Katherine, were transferred from the chapel.

St. Katherine of Alexandria gave her name to the Catherine-wheel. In Alexandria she protested to the Roman Emperor about the worship of pagan idols. Fifty philosophers were brought in to argue with her.

The remains of St Katherine's Chapel

Because they lost the argument, they were all burnt to death. The emperor tried to make Katherine marry him. She refused and was heavily beaten. She was placed on a spiked wheel, but it fell to pieces. Her emblem ever since has been a wheel – hence the 'Catherine Wheel' firework. She was eventually beheaded. He body was taken to Mount Sinai, where the monastery of St Katherine still survives.

Over the north door of the church are two sculptures representing the heads of Thomas Weld Blundell and his wife. The old cross in the churchyard was dug up in a nearby field in 1870. Until the 1930s, the church had a spire. This was removed when it became unsafe.

Walk down Hall Lane until reaching a signpost on the right, pointing towards Lollies Bridge. Follow the path as it curves upwards around to the left. At the top of the hillock, it swings right down to the rails of the racetrack. Cross the track by means of the two stiles. Continue along the edge of the rails to cross the track again by two stiles. Keep to the right-hand edge of the field, until reaching Lydiate Hill Bridge. Cross the bridge.

2. Turn left along the path on the canal (opposite to the tow path). This eventually passes through a small wooded area to come out in front of the canal cottages. Go straight on down the wide access road.

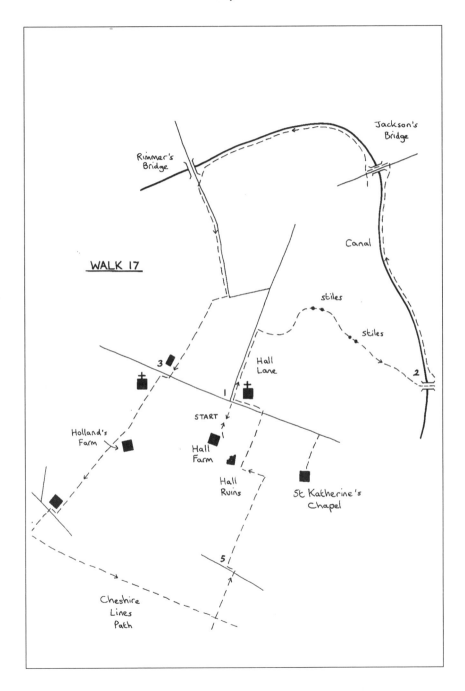

WALK 17

Jackson's Bridge

Rimmer's Bridge

Canal

stiles

stiles

3

Hall Lane

1

START

Holland's Farm

Hall Farm

Hall Ruins

St Katherine's Chapel

5

Cheshire Lines Path

2

Coming onto Pygons Hill Lane, turn left over the bridge and left again down onto the canal tow path. Continue on this until arriving at Rimmer's swing bridge. Turn left along tarmacked Eager Lane. As the lane bends sharply to the left, turn right along the footpath. This bends left, then straightens out along the right-hand bank of the stream. It emerges onto Southport Road, through the edge of the garden of what was once Church View Farm. It is possible to shorten the walk at this point by turning left back to Old Hall Farm.

3. Otherwise, turn right along the main road then left into Church Lane. St Thomas's Church of England parish church was built in 1840, the chancel being added in 1912. Previously Lydiate had been part of the adjacent parish of Halsall. Pass the burial ground and church hall on the left. Continue to the end of the lane, ignoring on the way the footpath sign to the right. With a converted barn to the right, go into the yard of Hollands Farm. Follow round to the right of the farmhouse onto a farm track. This takes you across the fields to emerge on Acres Lane by a cottage. Turn right a short distance along the road. Before the road junction, turn left through a gate onto a short track leading onto the Cheshire Lines Path.

4. From here turn left to follow the path back towards Lydiate. Pass over a path junction, with wooden stakes placed to prevent cars getting onto the Cheshire Lines. Immediately after a copse of silver birch trees on the left, turn left. The farm track soon brings you back onto Acres Lane. Turn left along the lane.

5. After 50 metres, there a signpost on the right, pointing you along the field edge. Arriving in the next field, turn left. Follow the edge of the field as it turns right by the side of the wood. This brings you back to the Southport Road. If you want to visit the remains of St Katherine's Chapel, turn right along the road, where you will find the entrance to the chapel grounds to your right. Otherwise, turn left back to the church and Hall Lane.

18. Maghull

Always close to the township of Maghull, this walk encompasses canal, old railway and fields.

Route: St Andrew's Parish Church – Canal – Cheshire Lines – Wood Hall Farm – Canal – St Andrew's Church.

Starting Point: St Andrew's Church Maghull on Damfield Lane, just off the A59. Grid reference: 376 019.

Distance: 6 miles (shorter route 4 miles).

Duration: 3 hours (shorter route 2 hours).

Map: Explorer 285.

By Train: From Maghull Merseyrail Station walk right along Station Road, left into Hall Lane, then right along Damfield Lane.

By Car: Parking available in car park immediately east of the church.

Refreshments: At the Running Horses pub at the junction of the canal and Bells Lane.

---

1. It is worth taking a moment, before starting out, to walk through the church grounds between the church and vicarage to the ancient building behind the present church.

This is the Unsworth Chapel, which is the only remaining part of the old parish church. It was built in the 13th century. Part of an ancient mural and a 15th-century font can be seen inside. An extension in 1830 soon proved to be inadequate because of the growth of population. This necessitated the building of a larger church, which was consecrated in 1880. By then the old chapel was very neglected. After much controversy the Unsworth chapel and chancel were retained, with extra work to make the building self contained. Thomas Unsworth was a Liverpool merchant who bought the manor of Maghull in the early 18th century. A gravestone immediately in front of the chapel marks the burial place of Frank Hornby of Meccano and Hornby model train fame.

Retrace your footsteps to Damfield Lane and turn left. The very busy

A59 Northway dual carriageway has to be crossed. Do this by means of the overhead walkway, which will take you about as high above sea level as you will be getting on this walk.

Descending from the walkway, walk up Liverpool Road North parallel to the canal, soon turning left at the canal bridge. On the other side of the bridge go through the gate, down the steps onto the canal towpath. Turning left under the bridge, continue on the towpath. Carry on at Shaw's Turn Bridge, then pass under Westway road bridge. After the Green Lane swing bridge, notice the old canal cottages on the other side of the water.

2. At the next swing bridge, turn left into Bells Lane. Immediately to the left is the Running Horses pub. Journey along the lane pavement, with open fields on both sides. As the road swings sharply right, follow the footpath sign to the left into Upper Gore Farm. This is no longer a working farm, having been turned into domestic accommodation. Follow the main path through the centre of the buildings. This swings to the right, then left by a man-made pond. A hand-written sign points walkers to the right, through a stile by the gate.

Walk across the field, passing over a flat wooden bridge, towards the fence of the Cheshire Lines path. A stile gives access to the path.

The Cheshire Lines Railway operated between Aintree and Southport until 1952. After years of neglect, a local action group was formed when access to the public was threatened. Consequently, Sustrans Ltd (a walking and cycling charity) began to construct a route for walkers, cyclists and horses in 1988.

3. Turn left, reaching gates across the path. Continue straight on across the intersecting farm track. You are now on a wide tarmac road, used by wagons, when the land to the right was a landfill site. Part of it is now a section of the Mersey Forest. Across the field to the left are the Maghull Homes, who formerly owned this section of the walk. It was made a public right of way by means of a compulsory purchase by Sefton Council in 1999. When the road comes to a sudden stop, continue along the path laid by the council. Follow it to the left round the back of the houses into Sefton Drive.

4. Turn right across Sefton Lane, into Racecourse Road.

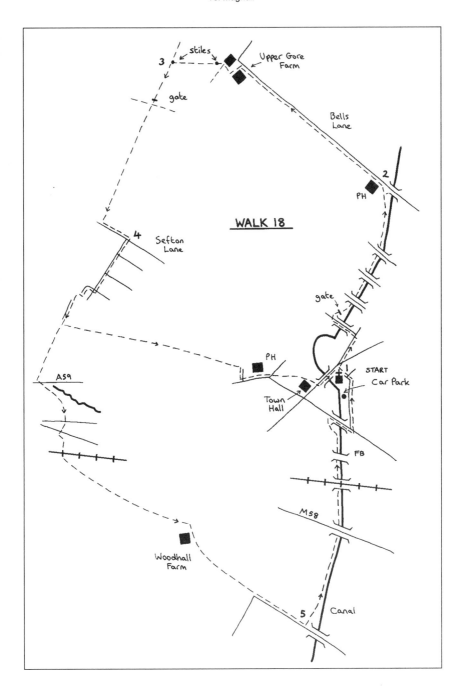

It was hereabouts that there was a racecourse before the days of Aintree and the Grand National. It may have originated from the days of the steeplechase between Sefton and Maghull churches. After a lapse of a number of years, racing was started again in Maghull in 1827. The inaugural meeting at the new course was in Aintree in 1829, after which racing went back again to Maghull in 1837 and 1838. The following year, it switched back to Aintree for what is considered the first Grand National. When Gainsborough Avenue, third on the left along Racecourse Road, was built, soon after the Second World War, the foundations of two of the old racecourse stands were discovered.

Opposite Gainsborough Avenue, turn right into Meadway, a cul-de-sac. At the end of the short road, go up the steps on the right. You are again on the track of the old railway. Turn left to pass over the former rail bridge. A footpath comes in from the left from the direction of Maghull High School and Woodend Primary School.

A. The short route is along this long stream side path to reach the corner of Ormonde Drive and Hall Road South. Turn left to the Meadows pub. At the mini-roundabout, cross to the other side of the road. Go across the grassland, aiming to the left of the Town Hall. Then ascend the steps up onto the A59. Turn left, over the canal bridge, to the overhead walk way and back to the car park.

B. The longer route continues straight on the main track, over another old rail bridge. The roar of the A59 is now very close. Go down to the footpath sign. With great care cross the dual carriage way. (You may feel it safer to walk left to the traffic lights. Cross the road. Then walk right along the road called Northway. As the road swings sharp left, turn right onto the dual carriageway pavement to arrive at the footpath sign).

Just to the left, another sign points to a gap in the fence. Follow the path, down the steps. Walk by the stream, until the path bends to the right. It passes a small copse on the left. Go under the tunnel. On the other side, follow the fenced path as it swings left to the foot-bridge. On the other side, the path runs by the motorway to soon turn right under the rail bridge. The wide path then swings left through the field towards Wood Hall Farm. Go straight ahead between the farm house to the right and the buildings on the left. Turn sharp right round the front of the farmhouse, joining a track

The canal at Maghull

between the hedges. This soon arrives at Brewery Lane. Turn left towards the canal bridge.

5. Just before the bridge go through the gate onto the towpath. Go left to pass a swing bridge. After going under the motorway and then rail bridges, pass a footbridge. At the next swing bridge on Hall Lane, turn right, then almost immediately left into Damfield Lane. Walk back to the car park on the left.

19. Melling

A gentle country walk on the fringes of Maghull.

Route: Hen and Chickens – Mossock Hall – Gerard Hall – Bridge Farm – Hen and Chickens.

Starting Point: Hen and Chickens public house, Melling. Grid reference 404 023.

Distance: 6 miles.

Duration: 3 hours.

Map: Explorer 285.

By Car: From junction 1 of the M58, turn left, then first left onto the badly signposted A506 Ormskirk road. The Hen and Chickens is on the right after a quarter of a mile. Note that there is no access at junction 1 of the motorway from the Liverpool direction.

Refreshments: Hen and Chickens pub for food and drink.

---

1. Go to the back of the car park on the left-hand side of the Hen and Chickens. In the right-hand corner is a gate and footpath sign. Through the gap on the right of the gate, the path runs on the left of the stream and hedge. Over to the left is Big Wood. At the end of the field, follow the waymark to the right. Cross the stream, by the sign to Spurriers Lane. Again stay to the left of the hedge. This is a long stretch. After passing a pond to the right, there is a wide track between wooden palings, which takes you on to Spurriers Lane.

Here turn left along the tarmac road. Pass a bungalow to the left, followed by Hesketh Farm to the right. As the road swings sharply right, by the house on the corner, carry straight on towards the gate ahead. A footpath sign, adorned with a 'Farm Watch' notice, points the direction. The path wends its way through a small copse, then between a row of trees on the right and a ditch and heather to the left. It then turns into a wide grass track, which stays by the ditch on the left.

Passing a footpath pointing left towards Cunscough Hall, continue straight on along the grass track. The motorway comes into view

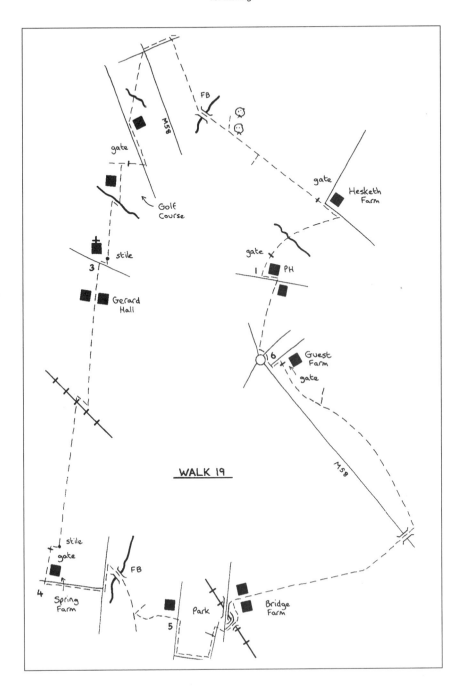

WALK 19

over to the left. At the end of the field, carry on through the copse. As the main track swings away to the right in the next field, stay on the right-hand side of the hedge. Arrive, after a short stretch of heather, at the footbridge. Then stay to the left of the hedge in the field ahead. Go up the steep steps onto the road ahead.

2. Turn left over the motorway, then left at the footpath sign, down more steps. The path runs to the right of the ridge, passing a small tree. Presumably there was a hedge here in former days. Coming to the other side of the field, the track passes over a stream. It then makes its way across the middle of the next field onto the road. Turn left past the row of cottages. Go along the road until you reach the sign for Mossock Hall Golf Club. Turn right past the footpath sign to follow the tarmac entrance road. After the open gates, follow the road as it swings left across the golf course. Take notice of the sign suggesting that you make sure that you give way to golfers on the fairways.

Go past the shop and club house, which are to your right. Cross the stream. Then, with a house in front on you, follow the waymark to the right. Walk along the left edge of the stream. At the next way marker, turn left along the edge of the golf course, with a ditch to your right. Ignore a large board announcing out of bounds because of organic crops. You are still on the public right of way. Eventually, after a high mound on your left and St Mary's Roman Catholic Church on the right, a stile brings you onto the road.

3. Turn right, then left by the footpath sign opposite to the church. Pass Mount Cottage and a bungalow. Follow the path straight through the buildings of Gerard Hall Farm. It passes over stone sets, then quickly becomes a wide farm track. This heads towards the railway. Before reaching it, the track bends a little to the right, to run along the right edge of a ditch. At the railway, turn right along the edge of the embankment. Turn left through the underpass to follow the farm track across the centre of the field. As the track passes the fence of the paddock at the rear of Spring Farm, the road is only about 100 metres ahead. For some reason this is not a right of way. To follow this, go over the stile in the paddock fence. Aim for the gate, between two outbuildings, on the opposite side of the paddock. Then turn left to pass in front of the house onto the road.

The Bootle Arms, Melling

4. Turn left along Brookfield Lane. On reaching Elm Cottage on the left, follow the road round to the left. Oppose to the notice for 'Moorcroft – The Cottage', follow the footpath sign onto the track across the field. Cross the bridge over the stream. Continue through the gate, with the 'Footpath Only' sign to its left. Keep on the tarmac lane until reaching a road going off to the left. Half right of this, a sign points to 'Park Lane ½ mile'. The path goes through a small copse into a field. Turn left, staying to the right of the hedge. In the next field, walk between the hedge and the fence on the right. The path then runs to the left of the next field edge, with a wooden fence on the left.

5. Coming on to Park Lane, turn right, then left into Douglas Drive. Second left into Mersey Avenue brings you past a park on the left. As you continue along the Avenue, look for a footpath sign between the houses on the right. This will bring you onto School Lane. Having crossed the road, turn left. Go through the bollards across the old railway bridge, to the right of the present one.

At Bridge Farm, turn right off the road. Walk between the shed to the

right and the farm house to the left. The tarmac track becomes a concrete one. Beyond the house, the wide farm track goes across a big
field towards the mast ahead. Through the gate, a footpath sign
stands at the junction of the lanes. Cross the motorway bridge
ahead. On the other side of the bridge, follow the sign pointing left
to 'Giddygate Lane ½ mile'. The track to the right is private. The
farm track meanders through the fields, parallel to the motorway. A
ditch runs along the left-hand side of the track. As it swings right
towards Guest Farm, follow the footpath sign ahead between the
ditch and wire fence.

6. Arriving at Giddygate Lane, turn left through the gate. Then follow
the road right up to the motorway junction. Turn right. Next cross
the dual carriageway to the opposite side of the road. Turn left.
Immediately beyond the 'No entrance' sign onto the motorway slipway, turn right down the bank. The path ahead is actually Maghull
Lane, the old road into Maghull until cut off by the motorway. There
is a little tarmac at first to prove this. The path runs between what
used to be the old road hedges. The old road reappears adjacent to
Lyons Farm. It is now only a few metres onto the main road. Here
turn left back to the Hen and Chickens.

20. Ness

A Deeside walk which passes an old hall and an ancient church.

Route: Ness Gardens – Denna Hall – Burton – Ness Gardens.

Starting Point: Car Park at Ness Gardens. Grid reference 306 756.

Distance: 3 miles.

Duration: 2 hours.

Map: Explorer 266.

By Car: Exit at junction 4 from the M53. Follow the Ness Gardens signs for 6 miles. When the signs cease in Neston, continue to follow the A540 for 1 miles through Little Neston and Ness.

Refreshments: At Ness Gardens, plus toilets.

---

1. From the car park, return to the main road. Turn right (the road sign points to Chester) along the pavement on the other side of the road. Pass a walled pond on the left and the Burton nameplate. By the bus turnaround, turn right down Denhall Lane. The narrow road affords good views across the Dee Valley as it wends its way downhill, with the odd house to the left. After crossing the rail bridge, pass the thatched Orchard Cottage and a pink painted house on the right to arrive at the T-junction on the front.

Turn right at the footpath sign to follow the tarmac path past the 'No access except for footpath' sign. The shore is a nature reserve. A notice always warns of firing when the red flag is flying. After the end of the stone walls of the Hall, come to the remains of an old chapel. A plaque on the door of one of the two cottages immediately next to the chapel commemorates Miss Stott, who made a bequest that enable the setting up of the Wildlife Nature Reserve. From here return along the path to the junction with Denhall Lane, but this time continue along the front, bearing left at the no entry sign on the right.

This is Station Road. Going uphill, the area of the old station can be seen to the left of the railway bridge. This is now Station House

Nursery, the station house being immediately to the left of the road. Soon, pass Greenacre bungalow and a sign to Burton Point Farm and Dovecote Nurseries on your right-hand side. Ahead can be seen the heights of Burton Wood. Just past Parkgate pony sanctuary is Hampston's Well.

The area was landscaped and restored in 1975. It supplied water to the Iron Age settlement at Burton Point and, much later, to the Anglo-Saxon settlement at Burton just before the end of the first century. It was formerly known as Patrick's Well. No washing of clothes was allowed in it. Once a year all the men of the village had to clean it out. By the 19th century, the well was named after a prominent local family.

Continue along Station Road. Turn left up the steps, just before the junction with the main road.

2. Having reached the bus stop on the pavement at the top of the path, opposite to the entrance to Bank House, walk to the left. On the opposite side of the road is a footpath sign. Follow this through the kissing gate. Go a short distance uphill, where the path swings to the right into the woodland. Keep to the low path, ignoring all going off to the left. The path is never far away from the backs on house on the right. Eventually arrive at a footpath sign, near to the Burton Wood signboard.

Another short detour is possible here. By taking the path to the right, arrive at the main road by a thatched cottage. Proceed right down the road. On the left is the entrance to Burton Manor. A previous house on the site was at once the home of the poet and playwright William Congreve (1670-1729). The Congreves were lords of the manor at Burton Hall from 1806 until 1902. The Manor was rebuilt in 1906 by Henry Gladstone, son of the Liverpool-born Liberal Prime Minister. It is now used for conferences. Almost directly opposite is Bishop Wilson's thatched cottage. Born here in 1663, Wilson rose from a farmer's son to Bishop of Sodor and Man.

Retrace your steps to the Burton Wood signboard. Continue through the wood.

On the left is the grave of two 16th-century Quakers, according to the

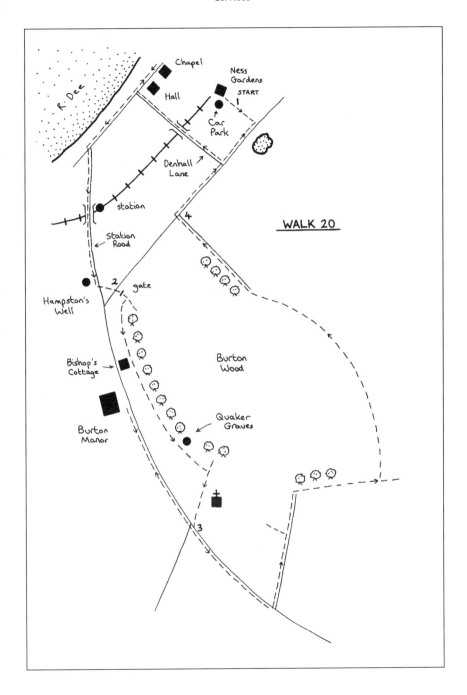

WALK 20

plaque on the stone wall, a tribute to men and women who adopted a 'courageous attitude in difficult times'. At the T-junction at the end of the path, turn right path down the steps into the churchyard. On the tower of St Nicholas church, built in 1721, is a clock with one hand. Because clocks were so unreliable in those days, it was a miracle to get the right hour, without worrying about the minutes. The clock was put right by checking it against the sundial. There is one to be seen to the south of the church. Inside the church, on the back wall, in a glass case, is a book of prayers and meditations by Thomas Wilson, the afore-mentioned Bishop of Sodor and Man. He started a school in Burton in 1724. The present school still bears his name.

On the wall of the north aisle are memorials to the Congreve family. On the wall of the south aisle is the hatchment replete with the coat of arms of the Congreve and Birch families. On the same wall is a bible box to which Bibles were chained, because they were so scarce. Near to it is a 16th-century edition of Foxe's *Book of Martyrs*. At the far end of the north aisle is the 14th-century Massey Chapel. This is the only surviving part of the pre 1721 building. The Massey family came from nearby Puddington and were the biggest landowners in the area. The 17th communion rails in the south aisle are reputed to be the oldest in the Wirral. The window behind the altar is the work of Charles Kempe, with his distinctive wheatsheaf motif in the left corner.

3. From the church go through the main gates, opposite to where you came into the churchyard. On reaching the road, turn left and then left again, at the war memorial, onto a wide track. A footpath sign points the direction, while a notice warns that only residents' vehicles are allowed. After passing another footpath sign pointing to the left, arrive a Burton Wood National Trust sign. Turn right down a wide track, reaching a signpost denoting a cul-de-sac bridleway. Reaching the end of the wood continue along the well-worn path. With a fallen branch ahead of you, turn left along the edge of the field past a lone tree. After going under telegraph wires, turn right along the stone lane, passing another entrance to Burton Wood.

4. At the end of the lane (Wood Lane), turn right along the main road. There are extensive views to the left, before reaching the end of the walk at Ness Gardens.

**Ness Botanic Gardens
(by permission of Ness Gardens)**

Ness Gardens were started in 1898 by Arthur Bulley, a Liverpool cotton merchant. He was particular interested in Himalayan and Chinese mountain plants. He sent groups to the Far East to bring back plants, which were then grown at Ness. Bulley started the company of Bees Ltd, which moved to Sealand in 1911. He died in 1942. Six years later his daughter Lois passed the gardens onto Liverpool University, with the stipulation that they should always be botanical gardens, part of which should be open to the public. The gardens (admission charge) are open March to October daily 10.00am-5.00pm and November to February daily 11.00am-4.00pm. There is a shop. Refreshments and light lunches are available.

21. Port Sunlight

Not the first, but one of the best of the Garden Cities, a walk round Port Sunlight's spacious greenery and black and white buildings is comparable to a walk round a typical English country village.

Route: Heritage Centre – War Memorial – Lady Lever Art Gallery – Heritage Centre.

Starting Point: The Heritage Centre at 95 Greendale Road. Grid reference: 335 844.

Distance: 2 miles.

Duration: 1 hour (plus time at the Heritage Centre and Art Gallery).

Map: Explorer 266.

By Train: Port Sunlight Merseyrail station is adjacent to the village.

By Car: Coming from the West, leave the M53 at junction 5. Then follow the signs on the A41 to Birkenhead. Coming from Liverpool, use the Birkenhead tunnel onto the A41 Chester Road. Follow the signs.

Refreshments: The Bridge Inn on the corner of Church Drive and Bolton Road and the Lady Lever Art Gallery.

---

1. The walk begins with a visit to the Heritage Centre in Port Sunlight.

Port Sunlight was the creation of William Lever, the first Lord Leverhulme. Lever had moved his soap factory from Warrington to what was then an uninspiring and dismal marshland on the edge of the Mersey. His vision was not only of a new factory, but of a garden village to house his workers. Work started in 1888, continuing into the 20th century. The factory, enlarged and modernised, is still situated by the village named after Lever's famous soap.

The Heritage Centre displays photographs and old film of the pioneer village, which must have seemed like heaven to the workers, compared with contemporary industrial slums. The building was erected in 1896 as a hotel, but there was little demand for its services. There is also a

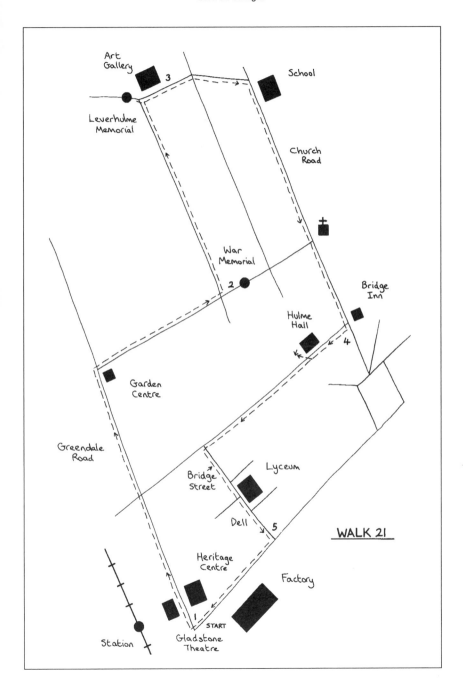

scale model of the village on show and plans of the time. The Centre is open Mondays to Friday 10.00am – 4.00pm, Saturday and Sunday 10.00am – 4.00pm (April to October) 11.00am -4.00pm (November to March).

Almost opposite the Heritage Centre is the Gladstone Theatre. It was named after the Liberal Prime Minister, W. E. Gladstone, who opened it in 1891 for use for recreational and dining purposes. It was the first public building that Lever had erected. In recent times its use has been as a theatre. Walk along Greendale Road, parallel to the railway. After crossing over Bolton Road, turn right along the Causeway, with the Garden Centre on the corner.

2. Ahead is the War Memorial to local people who gave their lives in the two world wars.

Designed by William Goscombe John, it has the theme of defence of the home. It depicts soldiers standing guard over women and children, a nurse treating the wounds of a wounded soldier, a woman shelters young children, and a Boy Scout shelters with soldiers. The panels of the monument are a memorial to the Red Cross, Military and Naval Services and the Anti-aircraft defences. From the memorial, the Lady Lever Art Gallery can be seen in the distance at the end of the sweeping vista of what is known as The Diamond.

Walk down either of the roads parallel to The Diamond, Queen Mary's or King George's Drive.

To the left of the Art Gallery is the Leverhulme Memorial. Designed by William Reid Dick, this was erected in 1930 as a tribute from the Port Sunlight workers. The crowning figure of Inspiration was on display before erection at the British Pavilion at the 1930 Antwerp Exhibition. The figures lower down represent Industry, Art, Education and Charity, all of which were concepts close to Leverhulme's heart. The Lady Lever Art Gallery was built between 1913 and 1922 by Leverhulme's own building department. Erected in memory of his wife, it contains much of Leverhulme's collection of art and artefacts. The paintings include pre-Raphaelite works by masters such as Millas, Ford Madox Brown and Rossetti, as well as English artists such as Constable and Turner. There are displays of Wedgwood china,

18th-century furniture, tapestries and Greek and Roman sculptures. Opening times are 10.00am-5.00pm Monday to Saturday. 12noon-5.00pm on Sundays. Closed 23 to 26 December and on 1 January.

Bridge Cottage, Port Sunlight Heritage Centre (by permission of Port Sunlight Village Trust; photo by Robert Baxter)

3. From the Art Gallery continue along Windy Bank, away from the monument. The road curves around, alongside grassland to meet Church Road. Along this stand school, church and pub, the three main constituents of most villages. Walking to the right, first is Church Drive Primary School.

The sunken playground to the left of the building shows that much of the village was originally built on land which had tidal inlets from the River Mersey. Leverhulme had started a school in what is now the Lyceum, but had this one purpose built in 1903. Next to the school is Christ Church. This is not, as it may look from its architecture, a Church of England parish church, but one of the Congregational (now United Reformed) denomination. This reflected Leverhulme's denominational allegiance. It was opened in 1902, having been built with Helsby sandstone in Gothic style by the factory's building section. At the west end of the interior is a Boys Brigade memorial, placed there in 1931. Nearly all the windows are memorials to members of the Leverhulme family. The foundation stone, marked 1902, is in the west wall inside the church. The Lady Lever memorial was built onto the external west wall in 1913-14.

Outside the northern end of the church is the enclosed founder's tomb. Here are buried the first Viscount, William Hesketh Lever (19 September 1851 – 7 May 1925) and his wife Elizabeth Helen (4 December 1856 – 24 July 1913). Alongside is the tomb of his son, the 2nd Viscount, William Hulme Lever (25 March 1888 – 27 May 1949) and his wife Winifred Agnes (11 July 1899 – 19 February 1966). The Leverhulme line ended with the death of the last Viscount in 2000.

At the end of the road, on the corner with Bolton Road, is the Bridge Inn.

Two years after its opening in 1900, Leverhulme held a vote whether it should sell alcohol. The villages overwhelmingly voted in favour. An extension at the rear was added in 1964. Originally there was a bridge here across one of the tributaries of the Mersey.

4. Walk to the right down Bolton Road. On the right you will come to Hulme Hall, which now trades in conferences and banquets.

It opened as a dining hall for women in 1901, having room for 2000. Hulme was the maiden name of the first Viscount's wife. A short detour along the left-hand side of the Hall will bring you to a memorial garden. At the front, with wide views towards the war memorial and art gallery, is a memorial to all those who died in the Hillsborough Football disaster of 1989.

After retracing your steps to Hulme Hall, continue right along Bolton Road, taking time to look at No. 20. A plaque tells that King George V and Queen Mary made an impromptu call here during a visit to the village in 1914.

Turn left along Bridge Street.

To the immediate left of the bridge is The Lyceum, which was erected between 1894 and 1896. It housed the school and church services, before purpose built premises were erected for them. The Unilever Archives are now kept here. On the opposite corner is Bridge Cottage, now the home of the minister of Christ Church. A blue plaque on the wall states that Leverhulme lived here from 1896-7. It was also used for a scene in the film 'Chariots of Fire' in 1981.

From Bridge Cottage, continue along Park Road and back along the other side of The Dell. It was also originally an inlet from the Mersey. It is now beautifully landscaped. The bridge was built in 1894 and sandblasted in 1987.

5. Turn right into Wood Street.

Through the openings in the original factory walls, the modern factory can be seen. Just before arriving back at Heritage House, on the left corner of Wood Street and Greendale Road, is Lever House. These are the factory offices, built with a classical style entrance in 1885. Over the doorway is the 'By Appointment' sign, a reminder of Royal approval in 1902.

22. Roby

Two parks formerly belonging to Victorian worthies and a new national centre make this walk of more than usual interest.

Route: Roby Road – Carr Lane – Bowring Park – Court Hey Park – National Wildflower Centre – Roby Road.

Starting Point: Bowring Park Golf Club and Picnic Area. Grid reference: 426 905.

Distance: 4 miles.

Duration: 2 hours.

Map: Explorer 275.

By Train: Roby Station, picking up the walk at the corner of Station Road and Roby Road.

By Car: From junction 5 of the M62, follow the A5080 to Roby and Huyton. The starting point is on the right immediately after leaving the motorway.

Refreshments: At Roby Kiosk on the corner of Bridge Road and Roby Road and at the Wildflower Centre.

---

1. Bowring Park was the estate of Sir William Bowring. In 1893 he became the first elected mayor of Liverpool. He bequeathed the hall and the estate to Liverpool City Council in 1906. Seven years later it opened as the first municipal golf course in the country.

Turn right on leaving the car park to follow the path going right. This curves round through the parkland to reach the Roby Road. Go right along the road, passing Derby Lodge.

Near the corner with Bridge Road, on the opposite side you will see the Roby Kiosk. Between Bridge Road and Station Road is located the ancient Roby Cross. Also at this point stands the white single story toll cottage of 1726, erected at the time when toll gates came into being in Liverpool. In those days, this was the main route between

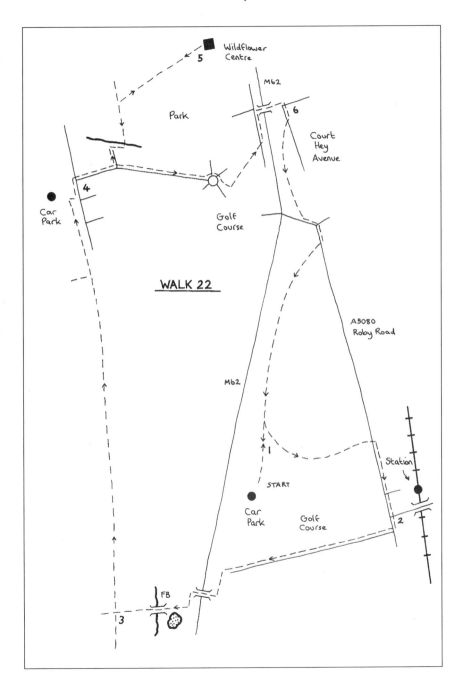

Liverpool and Warrington. On the other corner of Station Road and Roby Road are some beautiful old village houses.

2. After passing the entrance to Wychwood Park, turn right through the bollards into Carr Lane. The footpath sign indicates '1 mile to Netherley'. Start to descend through the deep wide cutting. As the path narrows between hedges, there is housing on the left and the golf course to the right. Eventually the path, now stone-based, swings left and right down to the footbridge over the M62.

On the other side of the motorway, the path goes to the left and then right. Keep to the right of the short length

Roby Cross

of high hedge. Cross the planks by the side of the pond. then stay right of the next hedge length. A bridge enables you to cross the stream. Follow the footpath sign, which points you straight ahead across a very large field. Stay on this until reaching a wide cross-track. As the narrow path continues ahead, turn right.

3. The track makes its way under telegraph wires and over a flat bridge. After passing between the high hedges, keep straight on in the next field. For a while the path is less distinct, but soon becomes a well used narrow grass track. This next runs to the right of a short stretch of hedge to arrive in a field corner. As one branch of the path continues around the edge of the field, go straight ahead on the path through the brambles. Go up through the fence, to walk along the right-hand side of the sports field.

4. On reaching the car park, turn right through the gates into Edenhurst Avenue. Turn left, then right along Gladstone Avenue. Next turn left into Glynne Grove. At the end of this cul-de-sac carry straight on along in the direction of the footpath sign to Court Hey Park. The path turns right along the side of the stream and left over a bridge. Follow the line of the school fence to turn right across the park to the far corner.

William Gladstone's brother, Robert, lived in a house here in the mid-19th century. When in 1878 the rail track through Roby was replaced, some of the original sandstone sleepers of George Stephenson's 1827 Edge Hill to Manchester line were brought here. They were used to border the driveway. Here is based the National Wildflower centre, which was opened in September 2000. The 35-acre park is run by the charity Landlife. The centre contains a visitors and garden centre, café, and shop. The old stables have been renovated and the walled garden reopened. The entrance for cars is from Bowring Park Road.

5. Retrace your steps across the park back to the bridge and through Glynne Grove. This time turn left along Gladstone Avenue. Coming to the roundabout, follow the footpath sign next to Sheppard Avenue, indicating 'Roby Road $\frac{1}{3}$ mile'. The path follows between houses, then swings left. On the right is the golf course. As the path gets wider, with trees on the left, allotments appear to the right. At the end of the path, turn left along the concrete way. Cross Roby Road and turn left. Opposite to Rimmer Avenue take the steps down to the motorway underpass.

6. At the top of the steps on the other side, turn right along Court Hey Avenue. Stay on the grass verge. A path then takes you to the right away from the road. This continues through a stretch of wood and grass land between the road and the motorway. A wide flagged path takes you through another underpass. On the other side, turn left up to the road. On the right is the path back to the car park.

23. Sefton

The ancient church of St Helen, Sefton is the centre of a figure-of-eight walk, which includes an equally ancient well and a bridge, which took 70 years to replace.

Route: Sefton Church – Showricks Bridge – Sefton church – Brook Farm – Mill Dam Bridge – Sefton Church.

Starting Point: Sefton Church. Grid reference: 357 013.

Distance: 4 miles.

Duration: 2 hours.

Map: Explorer 285.

By Car: The church is reached off the B5422 halfway between Netherton and Maghull.

Refreshments: The Punchbowl, next to the church.

---

1. The church of St Helen is one of the hidden secrets of Merseyside.

The oldest part is the 14th-century spire. Most of the remainder is 16th century. The interior has a 16th-century canopied rood screen, with impressive carvings. The canopied pulpit dates from 1685. Along with medieval stained glass and a 13th-century mail-clad effigy, there is a 'Treacle Bible'. The Molyneux (Sefton) family lived at the manor house, which used to lie south east of the church until the early 18th century, when they moved to their already existing hall at Croxteth.

Walk up Lunt Road, passing the Punchbowl Inn. Soon there is a signpost pointing to the right. Before passing the barrier into the field, it is worth crossing the road. In a few metres you arrive at the ancient St Helen's Well.

It does not look very ancient, being covered with a modern covering, badly in need of repair. St Helen lived ca. AD255-330. She was the mother of the emperor Constantine the Great, thought to have been born in Britain. She spent much time in the Holy Land, helping to repair the holy places. St Helen's chapel in the Church of the Holy

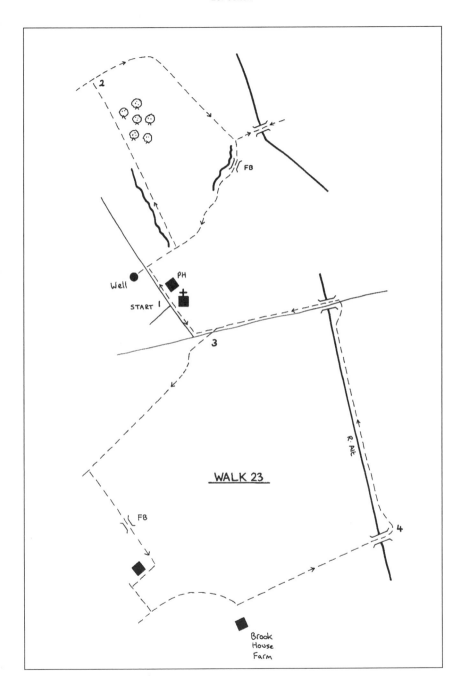

WALK 23

Sepulchre in Jerusalem commemorates the spot where St Helen was reputed to have found the cross on which Christ died.

Back across the road again, go by the barrier along the wide track until reaching Harrison's Brook. Turn left along the raised track on the right-hand bank. In summer the grass here can sometimes be quite long. Pass the wooden footbridge across the stream, which marks the route of a long since diverted footpath. At the end of the copse on the right, the tracks merge with another one. On the left are farm buildings.

2. Here, at the signpost, turn right into Moor Lane. Follow the wide track, turning right at the next junction. After about 300 metres turn left towards Showrick Bridge, which spans the River Alt.

In 1999 this replaced a previous one after a gap of 70 years. The original bridge was removed during the First World War for what were described as military reasons. No one is quite sure what they were, unless a German invasion was expected via Southern Ireland.

Retrace your steps to the waymarker pointing to the left. Follow the path over the flat wooden bridge. This area is part of the new Mersey Forest. Turn right, keeping the stream on your right. On reaching

Showrick Bridge

the farm track, continue back to Lunt Road. Turn left, back to the church. The first part of the figure of eight is now complete.

From the church, walk to the junction with the B5422. Turn left and cross the road to a footpath sign by a gate.

3. Through the gate turn right. The path stays close to the right-hand bank of the stream. It continues, veering round to the left through scrub land. Next turn right along a long straight track, through the fields.

On reaching a sign post in the field, turn left towards Chapel Lane. This is a field edge path, with the occasional piece of hedge, which acts as a boundary marker. Go over the flat footbridge, continuing along the field boundary. At the end of the field, turn right a short distance along the house fence. Then turn left along its drive to reach Chapel Lane. Proceed to the left, following the lane as it swings right and left by Brook House Farm, now a kennels. Over to the right can be seen the busy Switch Island, which is the junction of the M57, M58 and A59. Spare a thought for all those imprisoned in cars. Don't feel guilty about feeling how much better it is to be out walking.

4. Pass over the River Alt at Mill Dam Bridge. Turn immediately left along the right bank of the river to reach the B5422 at Alt Old Bridge. Turning left, it is now only a short distance, along Bridges Lane, back to Sefton Church.

24. Southport

*Although the sea keeps its distance, this most elegant of
resorts retains most of its Victorian buildings.*

Route: Lord Street – Seabank Road – The Promenade – King's
Gardens – Lord Street.

Starting Point: The roundabout at the southern end of Lord Street, at
its junction with Duke Street. Grid reference: 332 169.

Distance: 2 miles.

Duration: 1 hour.

Map: Explorer 285.

By Train: The station is the terminus for the Merseyrail service from
Liverpool. On exiting, turn left along Chapel Street. At the T-junction,
turn right along Eastbank Street to join the walk at point 2.

By Car: There is usually room to park in the St Paul's Square and St
Paul's Street area. This is found by turning along Duke Street from the
Lord Street roundabout. Then turn right immediately after the United
Reformed Church.

Refreshments: There are numerous cafes and restaurants along Lord
Street.

---

1. Our walk starts on the corner of Lord Street and Duke Street, by the
roundabout.

It was just here that the history of Southport began at the end of
the 18ᵗʰ century. Until then, the main settlement had been in
Churchtown, a little way north. The area covered by modern Southport
was sparsely populated by fishermen and shrimpers. They were
nick-named 'Sandgrounders', a name by which local residents are still
known. In 1792, the landlord of the Black Bull in Churchtown, William
Sutton decided to build a bathing hut, near the spot on which you are
standing. He had the vision to foresee a gap in the market to attract
visitors to the area. It was known as 'Duke's Folly', because locals
thought he was out of his mind. He was nicknamed The Duke', being

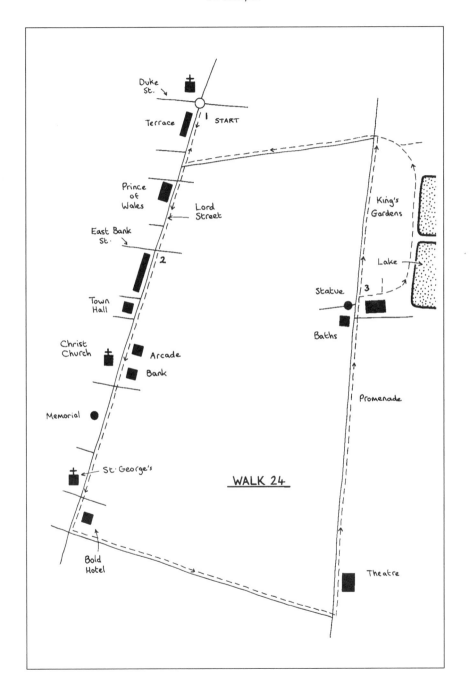

WALK 24

commemorated by Duke Street. Sutton went on to build his own cottage on the site. The story is that the building material was unloaded at a quay called South Port. In those days the sea came up to the present line of Lord Street, sometimes further. What was formerly an area of dunes and sandhills called South Hawes slowly became the large seaside town of Southport.

There are two large plaques on the apex of the green facing the roundabout. It was on this spot that Duke's Folly stood. One plaque records 'In the year of our Lord 1792 this house was built in memory of D.W. Sutton of North Meols, who was the first Founder and Executor of South Port, which was called his folly for many years, and it proves his foresight and his wisdom which should be remembered with gratitude by the lords of the manor and the inhabitants of this place also.'

Sutton's cottage was demolished in 1854. It was decided to commemorate it by the erection of a lamp in his memory in 1860. The second plaque you see was originally on the lamp. This column was erected AD 1860 by the improvement Commissioners as a tribute of respect to the late William Sutton commonly known as the Old Duke, the founder of Southport. He erected almost upon this spot in AD 1792 the first house in what is now the flourishing town of Southport, then a wilderness of sandhills.

The cottage was demolished so that a new planned street could be laid out in the 1820s on land belonging to two local squires, Lords Bold-Houghton and Fleetwood-Hesketh. Hence the name Lord Street.

On the corner of Duke Street and Lord Street West stands the United Reformed, formerly Congregational, church. In Gothic Style, it was built in 1874.

Start the walk up Lord Street by keeping to the right of the parkland. On your right is a row of white cottages, called Wellington Terrace.

These date from 1816, marking the Duke of Wellington's victory at Waterloo. They are the oldest buildings on Lord Street. On the opposite side of the road, the tall tower indicates what was the Cheshire Lines Railway terminus. This was once one of three stations

The Prince of Wales Hotel

in Southport, the only remaining one being in Chapel Street. The line ran from Liverpool via Aintree. The station was in operation, except for two years during the First World War, from 1888 until 1952. After service as a bus station, it is now a supermarket.

On the far corner of Portland Street stands the Prince of Wales Hotel, with the feathers emblem facing the street. In 1876, it replaced the old Union Hotel. It boasts being an early recipient official approval by the Royal Automobile Club. Over Market Street, you will come to the bandstand, a modern replacement of the Victorian one. On the right is the cinema building, formerly the Picturedrome opened in 1910.

2. Crossing Eastbank Street, you come to the most impressive group of buildings in the town. In front of them is the Information Centre.

The first is the Atkinson Art Gallery and Library. Notice the carved medallion over the doorway. Built 1876-8, the sandstone building was financed by William Atkinson, a generous local cotton merchant, who had a house on the Promenade. The upper floor has panels instead of windows.

Next to it is the Southport Arts Centre. This was opened in 1972 by the Duchess of Teck, later Queen Mary, as Cambridge Hall for use for public gatherings. The tower is 132ft high. Pass the entrance to the Cambridge Arcade. Lying back from the street is the two-storey Town Hall. Originally a private house built in Classical style, it dates from 1853. It displays the emblems of Justice, Mercy and Truth. In front of this cluster of buildings, lie the Municipal Gardens, where the Victorian bandstand was sited. The gardens were taken into public ownership in the middle of the 19th century. They were laid out in the present form 50 years later.

On the opposite side of the road to the Art Gallery, there is a building of temple-like proportions. 'Quid Pro Quo' is the motto high up on its front. It was opened as a bank in 1924. The Portland stone, Roman columns and huge door made of bronze did make it seem that your money was safe there. Beyond Corporation Street is the parish church of Christ Church. Originating from 1821, a chancel and transept was added in 1856. In 1862, William Atkinson donated the money for a gothic west front and spire. After the fabric was found to be unsafe at the end of the 20th century, much of the church was rebuilt.

Over on the west side of Lord Street, opposite to Christ Church, are a number of interesting buildings. The entrance to the Wayfarers (formerly Leyland) Arcade leads into a miniature Crystal Palace of glass and galleries. Built in 1898, it is an excellent stopping off place for coffee. Immediately next to it is what is known as the Muslim Buildings. This is not because of any religious connection, but because of its mosque like appearance, particularly before its dome was taken down. The shapes of the upper windows still help give an indication of the reason for the name. The Albany Buildings shift the architectural style to the time of good Queen Bess. Erected in 1884, the black and white roof projections are mock Elizabethan. On the corner of Nevill Street, is the old Midland Bank, now a book shop. After a taste of the Muslim and Elizabethan era, we now have Roman style. A look up locates a statue of Neptune. Inside, the building is just one storey. All along this section of Lord Street are the cast iron canopies for which it is famous.

Back on the Christ Church side, you will next arrive at London Square, which leads into London Road.

The outstanding feature here is the War Memorial. In the centre is an Egyptian-style obelisk. On either side of it in the square are two identical colonnades, bearing the names of the war dead. The emblazoned motif is 'To famous men all earth is sepulchre'. All of this cost £30,000 in 1919. Carry on, passing the Nat. West Bank and Post Office in a row of Victorian buildings. The church you then go by is St George's. It is United Reformed (formerly Presbyterian) built in Gothic style in 1874. At the Hill Street junction you will find toilets. On the far side, standing back from the road is a terrace of Regency houses.

At Union Street, cross to the other side of Lord Street.

In front of you is the Bold Hotel. Built in 1830, it is one of the oldest hotels in the town. Immediately to the right of the Hotel is Seabank Road. Follow this down to the Promenade. This was built in 1934 by Peter Hesketh Fleetwood.

An optional short detour by turning right will bring you to the old Promenade hospital on the right-hand corner of the roundabout.

The hospital was erected on the site of a previous hospital, which was opened as a place of convalescence by the Earl of Derby in 1885. It was financed by money left over in the Lancashire Cotton Relief Fund.

Turn left from Seabank Road along the Promenade.

Over to the right is the northern Marine Lake. It was constructed in 1892, five years after the southern part, being extended in 1963. Opposite to the modern Southport Theatre, is the stone built former Queen's Hotel, erected in 1866. Walk on along the Promenade to the junction with Nevill Street. On the near corner are the old Victoria Baths. These were opened in 1872 on the site of the previous baths. Although now used for other purposes, the building still bears the original sign 'Victoria Sea Water Baths. Entirely new Turkish, Russian & Swimming Baths. Finest in District'.

Holding pride of place in the centre of the Nevill Street junction is the statue of Queen Victoria. When it was unveiled on 15 July 1904, it was placed in front of the Atkinson Art Gallery. Later it was moved to its present site at the suggestion of its sculptor, George Frampton. Across the Promenade from the statue is the Pier. First erected in August 1860 at a length of 1211 yards, it was extended in 1868 to 1335 yards eight years later. This made it second only to that of Southend in length.

3. From the tabernacle at the end of the Pier, there is an option of routes.

A. Turn right into King's Gardens in front of the charity kiosk and the map of the Gardens.

These were opened by King George V in 1913. Ignore the first turn left. Go straight ahead to the lakeside. Follow round left along the edge of the lake, passing the end of the bridge and the model railway en route. At the end of the lake, where steps descend to the right, turn left along the wide tarmac path. Then walk left again to go up the slope to the road above. Cross over to turn right and immediately left down Kingsway. This brings you back to Lord Street. Turn right back to your starting point.

B. The alternative is to carry on along the Promenade.

Opposite to Scarisbrick Street is a memorial. This is to the 27 lifeboatmen of the Southport and St Annes crews, who lost their lives going to the aid of a sinking German ship, the Mexico, on 9 December 1886. There is a similar memorial in the Alpine Gardens in Lytham St Annes.

At the end of the Promenade, turn left into Kingsway to go back to Lord Street. Turn right back to your starting point.

More information about Southport is available in *The Treasures of Lancashire* by N. Bilsborough (1989), *Southport in Focus* by Catherine Rothwell (1991), *Southport* by Jack Smith (1995) and *Southport: A pictorial history* by Harry Foster (1995).

25. Tarbock

Fields and farms feature on this quiet country walk.

Route: Brickwall Inn – Tarbock Hall – Yew Tree Farm – Spring Farm – Green's Bridge Farm – Brickwall Inn.

Starting Point: Brickwall Inn, which has a large car park. Grid reference 462 876.

Distance: 5 miles.

Duration: 2 hours.

Map: Explorer 275.

By Car: The inn is situated on the B5178 between Netherley and Widnes.. From junction 6 of the M62, take the A5080 towards Huyton, turn first left at the traffic lights into Whitefield Lane. At the T-junction turn left along Netherley Road.

Refreshments: Brickwall Inn.

1. Leaving the car park, cross to the footpath on the other side of Netherley Road. Turn left to continue past the junction with Greensbridge Lane. Just after Brewery House, turn right at the footpath sign into Ox Lane, an ancient highway about one mile in length. Would it be a coincidence that Brewery House and its farm are situated near to the pub? The warning notice of 'Private Road to Tarbock Hall Farm', plus the no entry sign on the gate, is only applicable to vehicular traffic. After passing two houses on the right, the lane winds its way through the countryside. Immediately after going through a section of woodland, it drops to an iron bridge over Ochre Brook. As two tracks go right into Tarbock Hall Farm opposite to a barn, keep ahead as the hedged lane begins to ascend.

Little is to be seen of Tarbock Hall behind its outbuildings. It can be glimpsed by looking back higher up the lane. The building is partly 18th and 15th century.

A tiny pond in a copse to the left is passed. As the main track swings to the left into a field, carry on straight ahead on the grass track to reach a stile. By now the noise of traffic will tell you that you are

The Brickwall Inn

approaching the busy Tarbock junction of the M62, M58 and Knowsley Expressway.

From the stile turn right onto the tarmac of a road, which was cut off by the construction of the junction. It was part of Dacres Bridge Lane, which we will come onto again, having negotiated the junction.

2. Turn left up the steps onto the pavement adjacent to the slip road to the M62. Turn right to cross the Knowsley Expressway slip road. Pass underneath the bridge, then across the other slip road to the Expressway. On the far side, by the footpath sign turn right and immediately left. This takes you through a wooden barrier, along a wide path descending by the side of the Expressway. Through the next wooden barrier, turn left along the remains of Dacres Bridge Road, closed to traffic.

On the left is the woodland of Skettles Bog, a historic contrast to the nearby modern motorway. Indications have been discovered in this area of buildings dating back to the Roman era.

Walk on over Dacres Bridge itself, to come to the traffic barrier at the end of the lane, adjacent to a small white house.

3. A footpath sign points ahead to Cronton Road, but follow the sign to

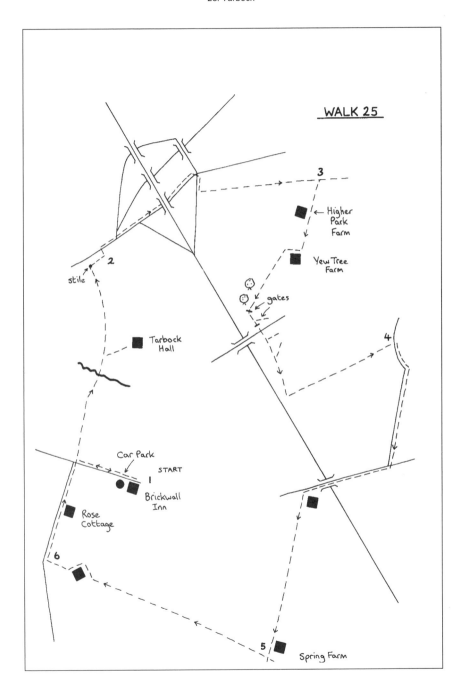

WALK 25

3

← Higher
Park
Farm

Yew Tree
Farm

gates

4

stile

2

Tarbock
Hall

Car Park

START

1

Brickwall
Inn

Rose
Cottage

6

5

Spring Farm

Water Bridge, which points along a lane. After a house on the right, the main track goes right, into the yard of Higher Park Farm. Go along the path, which is ahead, to the left of the outbuilding and farmhouse.

The track makes its way across open countryside towards Yew Tree Farm. At the time of my visit the farm was derelict. Just before the track ends, turn right by a small brick building, then left by another similar little structure. Now, with the farm outbuildings on the left, aim towards a hedge by a stream. Walk to the right of the hedge. At the end of the hedge, go into the next field. Walk across it towards another length of hedge by a stream, again keeping to the right of it. Follow the path as it curves round a small piece of woodland. Pass a wooden gate, to arrive parallel to the express way. The path goes along the edge of this to another wooden gate. Through this, ignore the path to the left. Walk underneath the Water Lane bridge. Again ignore all tracks to the left. Go straight ahead on the wide track, with the farm away to the left. After going over the bridge over a stream, stay on the stone path along the fence by the expressway. At first there is a high wooden sound barrier beyond the fence.

On reaching the telegraph poles, turn left along a wide grass track. The poles change from side the side of it, as you continue across the open field.

4. By a farm gate, turn right along Cross Hillocks Lane. This is a pleasant meandering country lane, which emerges onto Netherley Road by the Expressway Bridge. Cross the road, through the gap in the wooden barrier by a footpath sign. Turn right, noting the extensive tree planting on the left. Over the bridge, turn left by the footpath sign. Go down the narrow path and by the gate, which brings you onto another road cut off in its prime. With Cross Hillocks Farm on the corner, turn left at the footpath sign. After two houses on the right, the next habitations on the lane are the white Springfield Cottages. The modern large bungalow on the left, is followed by the more ancient house and outbuildings of Spring Farm.

5. At the end of the lane, the footpath sign indicates a choice of ways, Hough to the left and Green Bridge to the right. Opt for the right turn, which takes you, by the gate, onto a long stretch of farm track, along which the hedge seems to rejoice in alternating sides. Green's

Bridge plantation lies over to the left. At this point, to be so close the busy motorways and yet in the quiet depths of the countryside seems little less than miraculous. This piece of rural solitude ends at Green's Bridge Farm. Go over the stile in the wooden barrier at the end of the track. Turn left on a track around the far side of the converted farm buildings. Follow this, with the buildings and farm house to the left onto Greensbridge Road.

6. Cross carefully because of the bend onto the pavement on the other side of the road. Turn right, walking past Georgesons Farm. After a small cluster of houses, of which the oldest is one on the left simply called 'The Cottage', stay on the road as it passes the thatched Rose Cottages on the right and the lane to Dale Farm on the left. At the T-junction, turn right back to the Brickwall Inn.

26. Thornton and Little Crosby

The picturesque old village of Little Crosby is the highlight of this walk.

Route: Nags Head – Brooms Cross – Crosby Hall – Little Crosby – Nags Head.

Starting Point: Water Street, Thornton. Grid reference: 337 009.

Distance: 4 miles.

Duration: 2 hours.

Map: Explorer 285.

By Car: From the A565 Southport – Liverpool road, turn into Green Lane. Then left into Water Street opposite the Nags Head.

Refreshments: The Nags Head and Grapes pub on Green Lane.

---

1. On the corner of Water Street, secured behind railings, are the old village stocks and sundial. From Water Street turn right, then left again into Rothwell's Lane. There are houses and barns on both sides. After passing a field and Elm Cottage, turn right at the footpath sign opposite to Gamekeeper's Cottage. At first there is a stone track. As it bends to the left, this is replaced by grass. The path runs between a stream on the left and the boundary of Thornton Cemetery to the right. This gives way to an open field, with the path sticking close to the stream.

At the narrow tarmac road, turn left. Ignore a path to the left. Continue until the reaching a sharp bend in the road. At this point, leave the road to continue on the dirt track immediately ahead. The way is through open fields.

This is an ancient thoroughfare, because on the left is the site of the ancient Broom's Cross. This is where bearers would rest a coffin as it was brought on its way to its final resting place at Sefton Church. The spire of the church can be seen back across on the skyline. The original cross has long disappeared, but a replacement was erected in 1977.

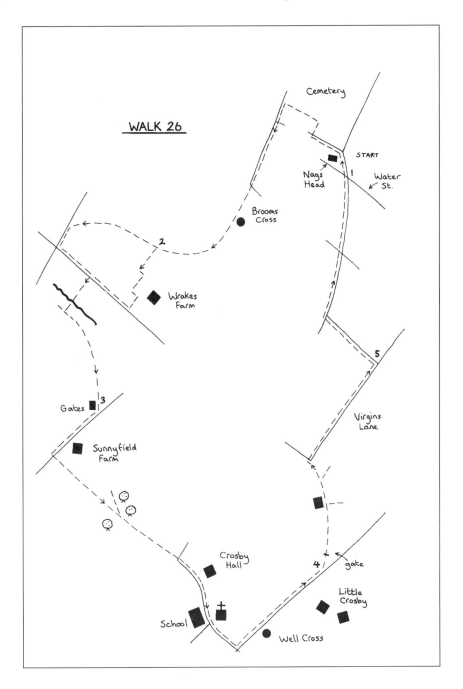

WALK 26

Cemetery

START

Water St.

Nags Head

Brooms Cross

2

Wrakes Farm

5

Virgins Lane

Gates 3

Sunnyfield Farm

Crosby Hall

4 gate

Little Crosby

School

Well Cross

Continue along the track, with a ditch to the left, until it becomes narrower as it goes to the right alongside a high hedge. After the hedge, the way widens out again, swinging right after reaching a byway sign. There are now ditches on both sides as well as the occasional tree or bush. Over to the left is Wrakes Farm.

2. On reaching a sign pointing left to Long Lane, go over the ditch and walk through the fields. (A longer alternative route is to continue ahead until reaching Lunt Road. Here turn left, then left again up Long Lane)

The path follows the line of drainage ditches. After a while, it bends left and quickly right again to proceed along a line of bushes. Then it does another left and right turn. From here it takes you to the junction with Long Lane, adjacent to a small coppice of trees. Turn right along the tarmac road, passing a pond to the right. Just after a single tree, cross to the other side of the road. The footpath sign points along a tree lined bridleway, which then has large trees on the left and a field to the right. After going over a brook, the hedged track emerges onto Park Wall Road.

The wall in question was built towards the end of the 18ᵗʰ century, enclosing the grounds of Ince Blundell Hall. The Hall, not open to the public, was built in 1777 by Henry Blundell. In the grounds are a Pantheon, Garden Temple and Church of the Holy Family.

Walk left along the narrow tarmac road, with fields to the left. The wall gradually begins to get lower, revealing stately beech trees. Following a pond and Lion Cottage to the left, the road reaches the junction with the busy Moor Lane. On the right corner are Lion Lodge Gates. Its details are from a 17ᵗʰ-century painting by Sebastian Ricci called 'The Marriage of Bacchus and Ariadne'.

3. Cross over Moor Lane to the footpath on the far side, turning right. Pass by Sunnyfield Farm. At the end of the hedge, immediately before the wood, turn left into the field by the signpost announcing 'Back Lane'. Join the farm track coming in from the left. Follow it along the edge of the stream and woodland. After a gate on either side of the track, the wood ends. The track, now stone surfaced, goes on through the fields, following a line of telegraph poles. This reaches Back Lane by a house on the right and coppice to the left.

Exit onto the road, through the small gate by the footpath sign, to the left of the main entrance.

Cross the road to the footpath and turn right.

The wall and woodland are part of the grounds of Crosby Hall, the outbuildings of which are passed along the road. The Hall is early 17th century. The Great Barn dates from two centuries earlier. Part of the premises are used by the Crosby Hall Educational Trust, which provides help for deprived and disabled children. After the end of the hall grounds, the high wall gives way to West Lane House. Originating from 1719, it was altered on at least two occasions during the 19th century, as the diverse architecture indicates. It served as the local Roman Catholic church, until St Mary's, next to it, was built in 1847. The windows and monuments make it very much a memorial to the Blundell family.

Ignoring the right turn into Moss Lane, follow the wall of the church, passing the little war memorial. Follow the road round to the left into Little Crosby Road.

Delph Road, to the right, led to the old quarry, now filled in, which supplied much of the local stone.

On the right is the Well Cross. This is on the site of the village well, marked the edge of the village common enclosed in 1857. On the other side of the road is a wayside shrine in memory of Francis Nicholas Blundell (1880-1936). Again on the right, at no 25, is the village museum. It is one of many historic houses and cottages in this conservation area. Particularly outstanding are the Priest's House, with the cross on the front and the last building on the right, the old Smithy.

Continue on the pavement alongside the wall, noting the cross on it, indicating the position of a wayside cross. On the other side of the road is an extensive view across the fields to the sand dunes at the edge of the sea.

4. At the end of the wall, turn left in front of the entrance. Notice the lions crest of the Blundell family again. Turn left through the kissing gate, where the sign points to Oakland Cottage. The path follows the wall, across a field, until it reaches a hedge with a path coming

The Lion Gates

in on the far side of it. Go ahead in front of the cottage, to follow the path again along the edge of the wall. At the next hedge, this time with a path coming in front of it, keep straight on. The path ends at Virgins Lane. Cross the road, turning right along the footpath. The only building passed is Cottage Farm.

5. At the end of the lane, go left into Brook Road. After this, turn right into Ince Road. Cross at the traffic lights into Green Lane. Soon after passing the Grapes inn, you are back the Nag's Head.

27. Thurstaston

Rarely out of sight of the Dee Estuary, the walk includes a section of the Wirral Way and the sandstone heights of Heswell Dales.

Route: Thurstaston Visitor Centre – Dale Farm – Oldfield Farm – Thurstaston Village – Visitor Centre.

Starting Point: Visitor Centre, Wirral Country Park. Grid reference: 238 835.

Distance: 4 miles.

Duration: 2 hours.

Map: Explorer 266.

By Car: From Telegraph Road (A540) turn down Thurstaston Road. At the T-junction, with the church over to the left, turn right to follow round to the left down Station Road. At the bottom turn left immediately before the old rail bridge.

Refreshments: Café at Visitor Centre and at Broadway Stores on leaving the Wirral Way.

---

1. The walk starts from the Wirral Country Park Visitor Centre, at one time the location of a railway station. It is well worth spending time here.

Thurstaston station was built in 1886 at the time that the line was extended from Parkgate to West Kirby. Thomas Ismay, the company chairman as well as owner of the White Star shipping line, lived in Thurstaston village. It is said that he insisted on the line going along the shore, so that he would not be disturbed. The ground on the river side of the Visitor Centre was the site of camps run in the 1920s by Lord Leverhulme, so that his workers from Port Sunlight could have a holiday. During World War 2, the area was used by anti-aircraft units.

The Visitor Centre provides information and advice on visiting Hilbre Island Local Nature Reserve, located about a mile offshore from West

The Wirral Way, Thurstaston

Kirby. Information on tide tables and permits for group visits to Hilbre can be obtained by phoning the Centre on 0151 648 3884 or 4371.

From the platform by the Visitor Centre, turn right along the old track. At the footpath sign, carry on along the same track towards Parkgate. After passing a water refining plant on the left, go under a bridge. Here is a choice of ways. The path on the left of the wooden palings is the Wirral Way going along between high hedges. The one on the right becomes a wider lane, before a short stretch through open land, bending left to meet the Wirral Way again.

(At this point on the Way, there is a signpost. It directs along the way to Heswall, but also to Heswall Fields, which is National Trust property, and the Beach. This latter is reached by means of following the wide track that runs closely parallel to the right edge of the Way. Further along it, a sign points right to Heswall Fields. The track continues close to the Way until it rises onto the embankment level with the Way. It is an alternative route, but can be extremely muddy after wet weather.)

Advancing along the Way, the trees on the right become more set back from the path, soon after passing a seat on the right. Pass through two wooden barriers. There are now houses to be seen on the left and another seat on the right. The path is hemmed in by

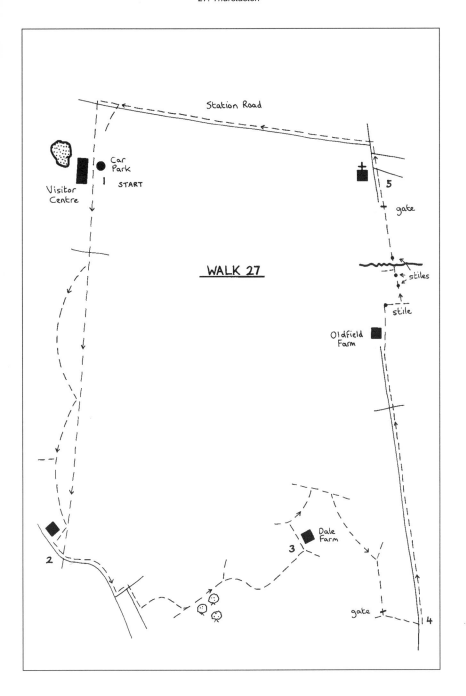

ferns. Then on the other side of wooden rails, the other path appears running parallel.

2. At a signpost pointing right to Banks Road, exit onto the road. (If refreshments are needed at this point turn right to Broadway Stores.) From the road, turn left over the bridge and the Wirral Way you have just left. Turn left into Pipers Lane, then immediately right into Bushway, which is a cul-de-sac. On the left, by the footpath sign, is the notice at the entrance to Heswall Dales Nature Reserve. The path ascends, with trees to the left and a separate bridleway on the right. After the two meet, go left on the main track that goes upward through the trees. Continue to follow this wide track as it first bears to the right and then to the left between wooden railings. Ignore all side paths. The track continues upwards through the heath land. Then it goes on a series of small up and downs. Soon after a stretch with a separate bridle way, Dale Farm comes in sight.

3. Immediately before the farm, turn left by a notice board onto a path marked 'Footpath only' which goes sharply down hill, along the side of a small paddock at the edge of the trees. Next, turn at right angles up the wooden steps, which take you along the other side of the paddock. After a short stretch through heath, the path comes to a T-junction by a seat. Here turn right. Then take the path to the right at the next junction. This eventually runs through trees to come to another T-junction. Turn right, with houses over to the left and trees to the right. At the gate, ignore all roads to the right. Go uphill to meet Oldfield Road at the footpath sign.

4. Turning left, you will pass Cleaver Residential Home and Oldfield Way and Gardens. There is then woodland on the left. Cross over Oldfield Drive on a wide track towards Oldfield Farm, noting the footpath sign directing to Thurstaston. Just past the farm houses and outbuildings, which are on the left, the track comes to an end. Make for the narrow path ahead, running between a stone wall and trees. The footpath sign at its entrance is sometimes difficult to see from a distance against the dark background.

This short path arrives at an old type of stone stile by a gate. Over the stile walk along the right edge of the field between the hedge and the fence. At the field corner, turn left to continue along the hedge and line of poles. After a barrier, go over a stile and down steps into the next field. Keep to the left of the hedge, with a wire fence on your left. After crossing two planks over a small stream, a barrier leads onto a kissing gate. Through this is a footpath sign, which as well as pointing back to Heswall and onto Thurstaston, indicates left – back to the Wirral Way – along the edge of a small stream. The route is ahead over a stile towards Thurstaston. Stay on the right side of the hedge to pass a redundant stile.

After a short stretch of hedged pathway, there is a choice of using a stile or kissing gate to continue on a wide grass track. The spire of Thurstaston church can be seen in the distance. Soon after going by another redundant stile on the right, the track becomes a stone one. When this swings right through a gate into a field, keep ahead on what is now a grass track again. With a parallel track to the left and a barn up in a field high to the right, you get to a gate and footpath sign. Go down the wide stone track, passing the farm, which is on the left.

5. At the end of the track, go left down the road. The parish church of St Bridget's is on the left-hand side, with a wide expanse of grass in front of it. Pass a road coming in from the right to quickly turn left into Station Road. After going by Old School House, the road becomes a country lane between fields. Proceed downhill, with the estuary in the distance, to arrive back at the Country Park Visitor Centre.

28. Thurstaston Common

A place of sacrifice is to be found on this stroll over the rocks and gorse of the common.

Route: Royden Park – Stapleton Wood – Caldy – Thurstaston Common – Royden Park.

Starting Point: Visitor Centre, Royden Park, Frankby. Grid reference 246 858.

Distance: 4 miles or 5 miles.

Duration: 1 or 2 hours.

Map: Explorer 266.

By Car: Leaving the M53 at junction 2, continue on the Upton by-pass. Follow the signs onto the B5139 for Greasby and Frankby. Soon after leaving Greasby, Hill Bark Road is on the left on a bend, adjacent to the Cemetery. There are no signposts. Travel along Hill Bark Road, looking for the Farmers Arms on the left. On the right is the entrance to Royden Park. Drive along the main drive to reach the car park. Here are toilets, the Visitor Centre and Ranger's Office.

Refreshments: Farmers Arms.

---

1. From the car park, follow the sign pointing to Montgomery Hill and Frankby Mere. To the right are open fields, to the left woodland. Follow the very wide track by the gate onto the road. Opposite is a sign post signifying Thurstaston. Montgomery Hill is a fast stretch of road, so cross to the pavement on the opposite side with care. Turn right. After passing some houses on your left, go down a wide drive way. Signposts point to Newton straight ahead and Grange to the right. At my visit, someone had reversed the signs to cause confusion. The one you want is straight ahead, keeping the railed paddock to the right. Pass Royden Manor and Birch House, which are on the right. After the last building on the left, Meadowcroft Cottage, the track swings to the right between stone walls, then left again along the back of the school premises. There are extensive views over the meadows to the sea on the right.

Arriving at a gate, go over the stone stile with steps. Now in a long narrow field, keep the hedge on your right. At the bottom of the

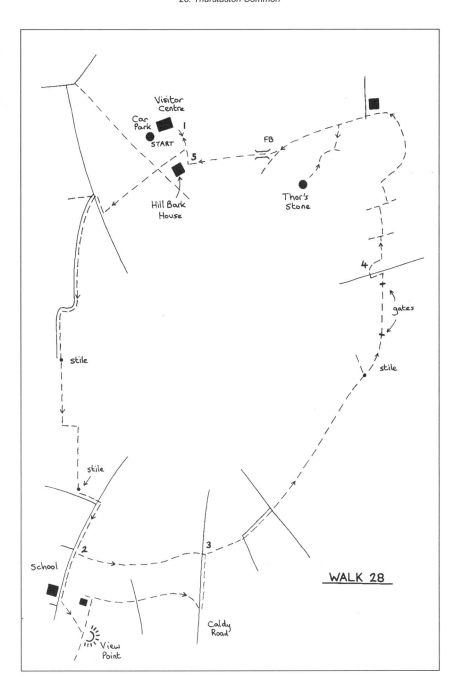

WALK 28

field, go left for a few metres, then over the stile and stream board-walk. Carry one on the path between the fencing on the left and the stream to the right. This eventually runs between the backs of houses. At the end, go over the stile onto Grange Cross Lane. Turn left, then right up Column Road.

2. Just after a house called Sylvan Lea on the left, there is a signpost pointing to Caldy Hill.

(**For the detour**: carry on up the hill. After passing the old building at the end of Fleck Lane, which is opposite to Caldy Grammar School, look for a footpath sign directing you through the gap in the stone wall. Ignoring the path to the left, go ahead. There follows a short sharp uphill section on limestone slabs. At the top is a view-point area, with extensive views across to North Wales.)

A plaque at the top gives the distances to places of note e.g. Moel Famau, 16 miles, the Great Orme, 29 miles and the Snowdon range, 40 miles. According to the plaque, it was erected in memory of Alfred Vaughan Paton MBE 1861-1930 by his friends. Paton made Caldy Hill available to the public in 1923. By walking a little to the right you can see in the distance Grange Beacon. We learn from the inscription that there was a windmill on the site until 1839, when it was destroyed by a storm. Two years later the beacon was put up as a landmark for ships on the river. The beacon is a little further away than it looks, as I discovered to my cost.

Back at the viewfinder, facing the sea, go left on a path that travels through the gorse. Do not deviate from this. At one point it passes over a wooden bridge, at another a sign near to a seat about a heath land project Go over a paths crossroads. Then, with a house just to the left, the path veers through bushes. There are a couple of trees in the middle of the narrow path at various stages. Soon, you emerge, through a gap in the stone wall onto a wide cross path, Fleck's Lane. Turn right along this. There are stones walls on both sides. As it goes down Caldy Hill, it crosses a road, King's Drive, to continue on the downward slope. It comes out on Caldy Road, by the bridlepath sign. Now turn left to walk down the road, until reaching the place where the footpath emerges from the Stapleton Wood)

For the shorter route, turn left up the steps. Keep straight on. In the descent through the woods, a path keeps to the wall on the edge of the wood. The other runs just a few metres above it. As long as you keep to the edge of the slope and do not turn up it, there is no danger of deviating off the path. The paths eventually merge just after passing a second seat in need of repair. Reaching the corner of the wood, stone steps go down to the left. Then go along the alley, with the fences of houses on the left and the wood on the right, to arrive at the road by a gate.

3. Directly across the road, a footpath sign points to Thurstaston. The path runs between wooden fences and hedges to reach the road. Turn left along Long Hey Road to the T-junction. Immediately on the opposite side of Croft Road East, a signpost points along a very wide track to Thurstaston Hill. Follow this through the fields and horse paddocks. As it swings to the left, there is a stile ahead. In the field, stay to the left of the fence as you go straight on. Through the kissing gate, turn left along the hedge. At the next kissing gate, emerge onto the road. Turn left along the pavement.

4. Cross the road to the footpath sign to Thurstaston Common, just by the sports field. The path takes you back along by the stone wall boundary with the road. Soon it veers left through thick gorse. On reaching trees, go straight ahead up hill at the crossroads of paths. The path emerges into the open, being a little indistinct over the last few metres, until it reaches the well-used cross path. Turn right along the slope of the hill, then turn left directly uphill on a short sharp climb to the top. At the top, pause on the limestone plateaux to admire the panoramic view. It makes the climb well worthwhile. Go right round the edge of the hill to reach a viewfinder placed in memory of Andrew Blair in 1923 by the Liverpool and District Ramblers Association. In sight of it is a trig point.

Walk on a little further. Then, ignoring the path to the right, go ahead down the slope to the end of the road, School Lane. There is a large red house to the right. At the road, turn left by the gate. Walk along the path, keeping the stone wall close to the right.

If a detour is required to view Thor's Stone, take the first path uphill to the left. The stone, 25 metres of red sandstone, is Wirral's miniature answer to Australia's Ayres Rock. The stone takes its name from the myth that the Danes made sacrifices to the god Thor at this spot. At a small rock escarpment, turn right towards the small mere.

Keep to the left of the mere to arrive at the Stone. Return to the bottom path by the same route.

Continue on the bottom path, which is joined by a stream between the path and the wall. On reaching the end of the stream, turn right over the wooden bridge. From here the path is straight ahead. It crosses a number of path intersections. At two of them, there is a stone in the middle. At a third, a stone just after the intersection. Do not deviate from going ahead all the length of this longish section.

5. The path ends at a T-junction, with a stone wall ahead. You can see the imposing Hill Bark House on the slope on the other side of the wall.

The remarkable thing about the house is that it has not always been on this site. It started life on Bidston Hill, until Sir Ernest Royden had it removed brick by brick to its present position more than half a century ago.

You may wish to go through the gap in the wall into the park land to get a closer view. Otherwise, turn right along the wide track. At the nature reserve sign by the beginning of a stone wall, turn left along the edge of the big field. This path brings you back to the car park.

Hill Bark House

29. Wavertree

This city walk takes in a mystery, the smallest house in the country and an old prison.

Route: Picton Clock – North Drive – Sandown Lane – High Street – Church Road North – Wavertree Park – Prince Alfred Road – Picton Clock.

Starting Point: Lake Road, Wavertree or on the left side of Mill Lane, adjacent to the children's playground. Grid reference 392 894.

Distance: 3 miles.

Duration: 2 hours.

Map: Explorer 275.

By Car: Wavertree lies on the B5178. It is most easily accessible from Childwall Five Ways on Queens Drive, the ring road, by taking the city centre direction. The landmark of Picton Clock will be seen after approximately half a mile.

Refreshments: The High Street contains enough pubs and restaurants to feed an army.

---

1. Picton clock on the roundabout and the old prison on the village green are reminders of Wavertree's past history.

Sir James Picton was the benefactor of the clock in 1884, while the detention centre for local vagrants dates from 1796. Walk along the edge of the children's playground until reaching North Drive. Here on the corner is Monk's Well. The base is many centuries old. As so often happened, it was the cross on the base that got damaged and was replaced in the 19th century. The inscription 'Deus dedit, Home bebit' means 'God gives, Man drinks'.

Walk through the gate to the left into the children's playground.

Until the mid-1920s, this was the site of a lake, fed from Monk's Well . It supplied water for the village. Immediately in front of you is a lone stone, known as the Salisbury Stone. The Marquess of Salisbury was the local landowner. He placed stones all round the lake, of which this one is the sole survivor. The name Lake Road relates to the green's previous history.

Before walking along North Drive, if time allows a detour is possible. Go up the green-railed Mill Lane or drive up at the end of the walk. On the left at the top of the rise is a house named Sandy Knowe.

In modern times the house has been extended into flats, but fortunately without spoiling the original building. This was built in 1847 by Sir James Picton, the clock man. He lived here until he died in 1889. In addition to the clock, he is also remembered by the Picton Library in William Brown Street. It was dedicated to him because for many years he was chairman of the Liverpool Libraries committee. When built, there would have been extensive views across the estate and surrounding countryside. Part of the estate opposite was, until quite recently, the site of Olive Mount children's hospital.

Continue up Mill Lane to the to the railway bridge. The deep long cutting is part of the original 1830 passenger railway, which was a world first. Stephenson's Rocket passed along here.

Walk along the winding North Drive. Just after a small copse to the left, on the right is no. 31, with the nameplate Urn House on the gate.

The urn theme is continued on the far-end wall of no 29. An urn is built into the brickwork. Urns from the bronze age were discovered here when the foundations were being dug for the cottages in the mid-19th century. Two of these found their way to the museum in Liverpool.

On the opposite side, a large house stands back from the road. The garden on the far side has a grassed tump, surrounded by stones that resemble teeth. These may be symbolic of the fact that here a local eccentric buried her pet dogs.

On the corner of the second end of South Drive is St Mary's C of E Church.

The original St Mary's was sited in Sandown Park. It had been consecrated in 1855 and a tower added in 1882. The foundation

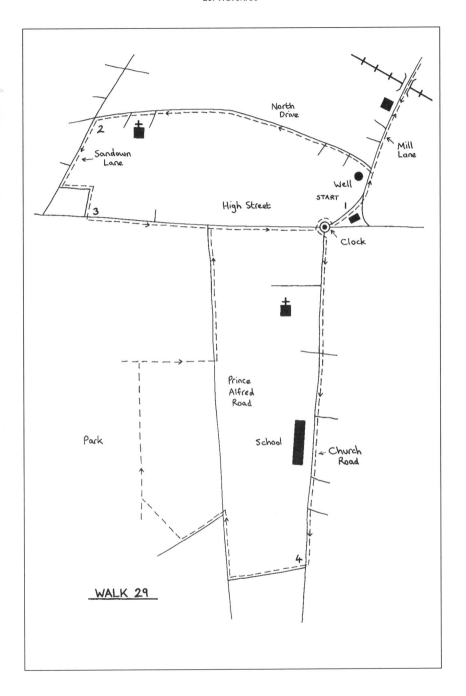

WALK 29

stone of the tower is on the east wall of the present St Mary's. In November 1940, the church was bombed. After using the church hall for services from 1940 until 1952, St Mary's moved into the present building, which had been a Methodist church built in 1872. Just down South Drive on the left is St Mary's Rectory, previously a coach house and stables.

Continue to the end of North Drive.

On the right-hand corner are early 19th-century houses, with distinctive fish scale slates. Unfortunately the splendour of the building is somewhat obscured by fir trees. Turn right along Sandown Lane with its sleeping policeman. On the left is a terrace of 19th-century two-storey houses, approached by steps. To the right is the fence of the ground of the cricket club started in 1892. At the junction with Long Lane are the lodge and one remaining gatepost of the entrance to Sandown Park. This used to be the estate of one of Liverpool's leading 19th-century families, the Hornbys. The 190-year-old Grade II hall was allowed to fall into ruin. It was demolished in 2000, despite all the efforts of the local conservation society.

2. Retrace your steps to the junction with North Drive, but this time continue down Sandown Lane.

On the left, standing back from the road, is the impressive and well-maintained frontage of Sandown Terrace, with Sandown Residents Association 1984 well advertised on the wall. Opposite is an old chapel built in 1837, but now occupied by small businesses. Turn left into Orford Street. This short street is probably the best conserved in the area, with splendid terraces on both sides.

Turn right into Grove Street until reaching High Street by the road sign directing to Victoria Park.

3. Turn right to reach the Wavertree Car Centre. Cross the road to the 1886 block occupied by the Post Office and the Chequers pub. A look at the iron grating over the pub door, reveals the information that the building was a branch of the old Liverpool Bank. From here go back along the High Street.

In front of an impressive terrace of Georgian buildings is a red phone

The old lock-up

box. Many such were designed by Giles Gilbert Scott. One inside Liverpool Anglican Cathedral, of which he was architect, serves as a contrast between his smallest and his largest creation.

Just past the corner of Orford Street, where you first came onto the High Street, is the 19th-century Rose Cottage, easy to miss because it stands back from the road. Adjacent to the cottage is a welcome patch of green. Opposite to Wavertree Gardens is the old police station. Opened in 1879, it remained in service until 1967. The rose emblem of Lancashire is above the doorway. It is now used as a restaurant. Wavertree Gardens were in their time a brave 1930s attempt to provide better housing for people moving out from the centre of Liverpool. The flats were built on the site of the tram terminus. A passageway to the near side leads on to the park. The flags on which you are walking were originally placed there for the trams, which in those days were, literally, horse-powered.

Still continuing back along the High Street towards Picton Clock, on the left is the Town Hall.

The Town Hall was built in 1872, but is now used as a pub. Over the main door is to be seen the crest of the Wavertree Board of Health.

Soon after this is one of many houses claiming to be the smallest in the country. It is wedged between The Cock and Bottle pub and a bookmaker. Built in the middle of the 19th century, it measures 14ft by 6ft. Opposite the mid-19th-century Lamb pub, on the corner of Waterloo Street. A restaurant uses the police station that preceded the previous one we saw. The end windows are now bricked up. Beyond the Lamb is a nice row of cottages, spoilt only by a travel agency extension.

You are now back at the starting point.

For the second part of our walk, cross the main road to the large brick building, now used as a supermarket. Its size and 1930s architecture gives the clue that it was a cinema built in the hey-day of film going. The Abbey closed in the 1970s. Cross over to the other side of Church Road North.

Here are two buildings belonging to the pre Victorian Wavertree era. Going along the road, away from Picton Clock, first of all is a cottage of indeterminate age, housing a funeral directors. Next is the oldest of the multitude of pubs in the area, oddly named The Coffee House. This attractive building is 18th century.

Cross narrow Hunters Lane. On the far corner, set in its own grounds, is the old Rectory, now used as a Synagogue.

Just before the traffic lights at the junction with Fir Lane are some gates, replicas of the ones which were there when Wavertree Hall was built. The 19th-century building set back from the road has been used for many years by the Royal School for the Blind. Immediately across Fir Lane is the church and graveyard of Holy Trinity. A large memorial to commemorate the fallen of the two great wars dominates the grave yard. On the other side of the road, an old mounting stone in front of the church hall is a reminder of the days when worshippers rode to church. Ironically, there is a bus stop immediately in front of it. The church itself was opened in 1794, the east end being refurbished in 1911, when the galleries were taken away and a new chancel built. At the bottom of the tower is a circular baptistery. The tower lost its surmounting lantern, when the latter became unsafe.

Proceeding further along Church Road, the Blue Coat school is one of the most prestigious in Liverpool.

From 1718 until the end of the 19ᵗʰ century it was housed in what is now known as the Bluecoat Chambers, off Church Street in the city centre. It originally dates from a few years earlier than 1718. The present buildings opened in 1906, with the clock tower being added in 1915. The cost of upkeep of the vast premises has caused the school to consider moving to another location. A story lies behind the three houses opposite, much taller in elevation than any of the neighbouring ones. They are known as Dilworth's Folly, after local builders who were anxious to get the job of building the school. The houses were built in the style that was to be required for the school. Unfortunately, the builders did not get the job.

From the school, walk along past the Liverpool Bowling Club.

4. Turn right down Barnhill Road. At the T-junction turn right. The park is now in sight. Turn left at the triangle into Grant Avenue. Then go right, through the park gate, onto the path.

The park was once part of the estate of a Liverpool MP, Samuel Graves. He lived in a large house, long since demolished. In 1895, the land became council property. Although officially known as Wavertree Playground, it is known locally as The Mystery. Why it is called that is part of the mystery. At the T-junction of paths, turn right. (For a longer walk go round the far edge of the park).

At the next T-junction turn right and out, through the gates, onto Prince Alfred Road. This was originally called Cow Lane, but went upmarket after the Prince had stayed with Samuel Graves. Go left along the road, passing the C of E Primary school to arrive back on the High Street near to the starting point.

(For more information about Wavertree consult the excellent book 'Discovering Historic Wavertree' by Mike Chitty, 1999)

30. Whiston

A country walk, close to the M57, mostly on reclaimed industrial land

Route: Stadt Moers Park – St Nicholas Church – Ropers Bridge – Pottery Fields.

Starting Point: Stadt Moers Visitors Centre, Pottery Lane. Grid reference 462 911.

Distance: 4 miles.

Duration: 2 hours.

Map: Explorer 275.

By Train: Whiston station in on the Liverpool-Manchester line. If arriving by train, the walk is most easily joined from the Health Centre on the north side of the railway bridge at point no 5.

By Car: From the junction of the M57 and M62, (junction 6) follow the Whiston turn off along Windy Arbor Road. At the town centre, turn left at the junction by the Horseshoe pub. Follow Pottery Lane over the railway bridge. The Visitor Centre and car park is on the left, just before the bridge over the M57.

Refreshments: Horseshoe pub, near the junction of Windy Arbor Road and Greenes Road.

---

1. From the visitor centre, follow the path towards the railway underpass. After passing through the barrier, turn right at the first cross paths. This takes you uphill. As it bends to the left, the path levels out. To the left there is a panoramic view across the St Nicholas' church in the distance. The M57 is in close attendance on the right. The way then starts to descend gradually, passing a couple of copses on the left. At the bottom of the hill, with the pond opposite, turn left on the wide tarmac path. Through the barrier, turn right towards the underpass under the motorway. The remains of the track of the old mineral railway can still be seen, a reminder of the days when the whole of this area was industrialised.

On the other side of the underpass, a bridge spans a stream. The

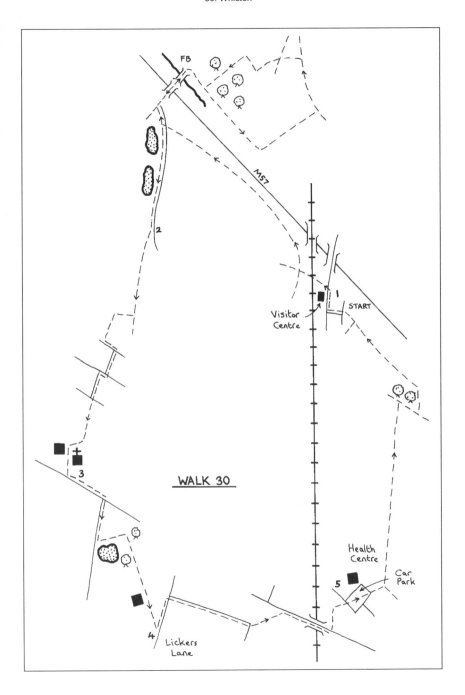

WALK 30

path then swings sharply to the right. Take the first turn to the left, which brings you through an avenue of trees. Ignore a path to the right. Keep on as the wood gets denser. A fence will soon be seen to the left, with factories beyond. A bend to the right follows, to bring you into open parkland with a children's playground visible ahead. Follow the perimeter of the park around to the left (no track), cross a path to reach another one. Turn right to continue on this path, which takes you to the left of the playground and across the middle of the park land. Just before the culvert of a stream and by a battered 'No motorcycles' sign, turn right onto a narrower track. This eventually bears right through trees. Continuing ahead, the motorway fence appears on the left, then the stream deep down in its culvert. Passing two paths going off to the right, stay between the stream and the woodland. You will reach the bridge that you pass over at the start of this loop.

Go back under the motorway bridge. Turn back through the barrier on the left along the road to the pond. This time, walk past the pond.

2. Now turn right along the narrower path. This takes you along the line of ponds. Coming to a grass triangle, take the path to the right leading into a large field. Turn left along the edge of the field, then left again, through the bollards, into the end of the Priory Close cul-de-sac. Turn right up to the road junction, then right and left into Mitre Close. This leads directly up, through the entrance in the brick wall, into the grounds of St Nicholas' church.

This Victorian edifice was built by the architect Street in 1864. In front of the building are buried members of the Willis family, who were the local landowners.

As the path bears right, turn left along the path to the back gate of the vicarage. Then descend the steps to the left, to turn right along the side of the church. This emerges on Windy Arbor Road, opposite the bus shelter.

3. Turn left and then right down a lane, with Saunders Nursery on the right and a lodge on the left. This is the entrance to Halsnead Park After a hundred metres turn left at a gap in the palings, by a white post. Go down the steps to the edge of the pond. Follow the path around to the left, then left again through the trees. Coming on to the

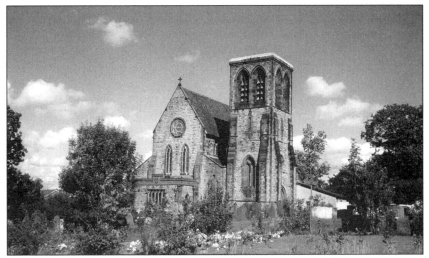

The church of St Nicholas, Whiston

recreation field, aim for the far right corner, to the left of the big shed.

4. Turn left along Lickers Lane, then right along Fisher Avenue. This ends in a cul-de-sac at Fisher Place. In the left-hand corner is a footpath, which takes you between the bowling green on the left and the school over on the right. This emerges onto the busy main road. To the left is the Horseshoe pub, if a stop is needed for refreshments. Otherwise turn right along Dragon Lane. This takes you over the railway bridge. This stretch of line became famous in the 1829 Rainhill Locomotive trials as the Whiston Inclined Plain. Stephenson's Rocket won first prize by being able to get up the incline without assistance.

Over the bridge, turn left at the bollards. Instead of going along the paved path, turn right between the houses on the right and the buildings to the left. This brings you out opposite to the Health Centre Building.

Turn right along the road to the car park. In the right-hand corner of the park is a gate, leading onto Pottery Fields. Stay on the right of the field, until reaching the footpath sign in the corner. Follow the along the path to the left in the Pottery Lane direction. This whole area was once the site of the Carrs Colliery. Stay on this path, ignoring all crosspaths. Go on to reach the point where the path goes up steeply through woodland. Instead turn right, then left uphill. At the T-junction, by two tree stumps, turn left. Stay on this path, with the M57 on the right. As the path goes uphill, with a fence on the left and a lizard sculpture on the right, do not take the path up the steps to the left. Continue as the track bends to the left, to drop down into the valley car park. Aim for the wide path on the opposite side, to the left of the brick building. This bears right to reach Pottery Lane and the end of the walk.

31. Willaston

An old deserted railway station gives the feel that a ghostly train will arrive at any time. A mysterious start to a circular walk in the Wirral countryside.

Route: Hadlow Road Station – Cherry Wood – Wirral Way – Hadlow Road Station.

Starting Point: Hadlow Road Station, Willaston. Grid reference: 330 773.

Distance: 6 miles.

Duration: 2 to 3 hours.

Map: Explorer 266.

By Car: From junction 5 of the M53, take the A550 south. From Hooton, follow the B5133 west to Willaston. At the village green, turn left down to Hadlow Road Station.

Refreshments: Wheatsheaf Hotel, Raby.

1. Before leaving or after returning from the walk, take a moment or two to have a nostalgic look round the station frozen in time.

Left as they were was when the station closed in the 1950s, the 1866 buildings are open to the public, including the signal box and the booking office. The latter houses toilets. A length of rail, plus the crossing gates, a signal and the milk churns on the platform all add to the air of authenticity.

From the station car park, walk back to the road. Turn right, to pass Rose Farm, Rose Cottage and Hadlow Terrace (dated 1883) to the left.

Two older houses from a time this area was farmland are worth noting. On the right is the cruck-framed Ash Tree Farm (1697), on the left Cherry Brow Farm (1739). Willaston Old Hall is 16th century.

The name Willaston means 'the homestead of Wiglaf', the village being the earliest known Saxon settlement in the Wirral.

Hadlow Road Station

At the end of the road you come to the village green, in the centre of which stands a beautiful copper beech.

This was planted in 1935 to commemorate the Silver Jubilee of King George V. Over to the right is the ancient Nags Head Inn. To the left of the green is the 17th-century former Red Lion.

Turn left along the main road. Cross over to turn right along a wide path marked 'Village Walk', which runs along the near side of Christ Church parish church.

Through the wooden barrier, go ahead on the short, wide concrete road between the church wall and the garages. Now navigate carefully. This is the one point on the walk where it is easy to go astray. Ignoring Elm Green on the right, turn left and then right, across the green, walking towards a brick wall. Getting closer to the wall, you will see a footpath sign, pointing through a gap. Follow the path as it goes to the left between walls and then along the back of some gardens towards the recreation field.

At another footpath sign, note Jackson's Pond on the right. Carry ahead, keeping to right-hand side of the recreation field. Over the stile in the corner of the field, carry one along the path ahead. There is a wire fence on the left of it as well as the hedge to the right. After the next stile, there is a fence on the right. Here, there are excellent

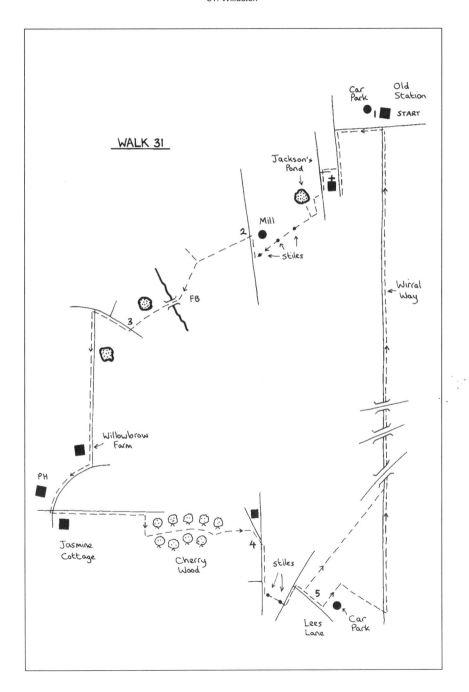

WALK 31

views of the old mill. Another stile leads onto the narrow Mill Lane. Turn right to pass the old mill.

2. Opposite to some old cottages and Mill House on the left corner, turn left along the lane, marked by the Raby footpath sign. The tree-lined path is an ancient one, about a mile in length. At first it is a wide dirt track. Soon after passing a stile and footpath sign on the right, the track gets narrower. At the sign indicating 'Benty Heath Lane' to the right, follow the Raby direction to the left. There are occasional trees in the centre of the path. After a wooden seat on the left, cross the flat bridge over a small stream coming in from the left. The path is now a stone one. Pass a pond over to the right. The path is then flanked by large beech trees. After another seat, the path emerges on the busy B5151, by a footpath sign.

3. Turn right along the road. Stay on the grass verge as much as possible. After the junction with Benty Heath Lane, turn left along Willows Lane.

The lane passes a large pond used for fishing. There are no houses along its length, until Willowbrow Farm is reached at the T-junction. Turn right here to head towards Raby. The first turn to the right is The Green. If refreshment is required at this point, turn right down to the 17th-century Wheatsheaf Inn. Otherwise turn left in front of the quaint, squat, thatched Jasmine Cottage. Over the stile by the footpath sign, go along the wide track, ignoring the left turn towards the farm buildings. The state of the track underfoot deteriorates as it becomes a farm lane, with grass in the middle.

The main track swings right into a field, but keep on the completely grass track ahead. Opposite a tree on the left, turn right over a stile, which leads you along a path towards the right of Cherry Wood. At the footpath sign turn left through the two old stone gate posts. The path runs along the left perimeter of the wood, which gradually gets narrower. When the path peters out, turn right out of the wood. The first short exit path you come across is an unofficial one, the second official one is very close to it. This takes you up to a wooden barrier, then onto a large field. Turn left along the edge of the wood to reach an exit in the left-hand corner of the field, opposite to Rose House.

4. Turn right to the road, then right again. This is a fairly busy stretch, so it is best to walk on the far side verge. Ignore the footpath sign on the left. Cross to the opposite side of the road, which soon has a pavement. After passing the large houses over to the left and the footpath sign at School Lane, look for a gate into a field on the other side of the road. Go over the stone stile by the gate and the partly obscured sign to Chester High Road. A few metres after this, there is another gate and stile. Then walk to the left of the hedge and later a stone wall. Another stone stile brings you onto the A540, opposite to Hinderton Mount Residential Home. Turn left and at the road sign to Little Neston, right into Lees Lane. Walk down this until you get to the sign on the left for the Wirral Country Park.

5. A somewhat muddy way onto the Wirral Way is to follow the bridle path sign, just before the entrance to the car park. Go along this tree lined path until reaching steps which take you up onto the embankment of the old railway. Otherwise walk through the car park. (There are picnic tables here on the grassland.) At the far end of the car park, turn right along the wide path. This reaches the Wirral Way at a T-junction. Turn left. The Way is very wide as it goes along the wooded embankment. This is due to renovations carried out in connection with the Millennium cycle route. Just after the steps from the bridleway coming up on the left is the narrow bridge over Cuckoo Lane. The inscription on the right near side of the bridge tells us that it was built in 1969 by volunteers from 106 Field Regiment of the Royal Engineers.

Continue along the Way, which later runs parallel to a farm approach road, before going through a tunnel under a bridge. Through the other side, keep to the track on the left, which goes under a small bridge and later under a larger road bridge. The track is now at the level of the surrounding countryside. A bridleway runs alongside it. After passing by a closed gate, the next landmark is a signpost on the left directing to Willaston, which is adjacent to a large pylon and a pond. Keep straight on. After a wooden barrier across the track, another barrier runs down its centre. The white crossing gates ahead signal the end of the journey. Before crossing the road back to the car park, note the steel sign post giving the mileage to Chester and Neston.

Also of Interest:

WEST LANCASHIRE WALKS
Michael Smout
No need to venture into touristy areas, it's all on the doorstep for Lancashire's walkers – "Knowledgeable guide to 25 rambles by the Ramblers' West Lancs Group Chairman" RAMBLING TODAY. *£6.95*

EAST LANCASHIRE WALKS
Michael Smout
The rambling reverend continues his revelation! This companion volume to "West Lancashire Walks" leads you to an abundance of walking and places of interest which lie just beyond your urban doorstep to the East – a haunted house near Warrington, an American Wood at Aspull, there's even a giant on the banks of the Mersey! *£5.95*

TOWN AND VILLAGES OF BRITAIN: LANCASHIRE
Michael Smout
The moors, valleys and mossland of Lancashire are the backdrop to this account of the county's towns and villages. "The histories of our towns and villages neatly gathered in one definitive guide" SOUTHPORT VISITER *£8.95*

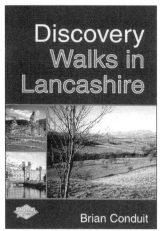

DISCOVERY WALKS IN LANCASHIRE
Brian Conduit
Walks with a heritage theme: Roman remains, medieval castles and abbeys, nature reserves, country parks and the many monuments to the county's role in the industrial revolution. "An impressive variety of walks ... rounded off with some fascinating details on interesting features" BLACKPOOL GAZETTE *£6.95*

All of our books are available through booksellers. In case of difficulty, or for a free catalogue, please contact: **SIGMA LEISURE, 1 SOUTH OAK LANE, WILMSLOW, CHESHIRE SK9 6AR.**
Phone: 01625-531035 Fax: 01625-536800   E-mail: info@sigmapress.co.uk
Web site: http//www.sigmapress.co.uk

MASTERCARD and VISA orders welcome.